# HOW TO BE A PEOPLE PERSON

# HOW TO BE A PEOPLE PERSON

## Márianna Csóti

**RIGHT WAY**

Typeset in 11pt by Letterpart Ltd., Reigate, Surrey.

Printed and bound in Great Britain by Cox & Wyman Ltd., Reading, Berkshire.

The *Right Way* series is published by Elliot Right Way Books, Brighton Road, Lower Kingswood, Tadworth, Surrey, KT20 6TD, U.K. For information about our company and the other books we publish, visit our website at www.right-way.co.uk

*For Nick – your patience and tolerance
are much appreciated*

Thanks to Isminur Mutlu-Smith for her help
with matters cultural

# CONTENTS

# 1

# YOU

Before you address the question of how you should relate
to others, which is covered in later chapters, you need to
know and understand more about yourself so that you
know what you are looking for in a relationship and *what
you have to offer*. This is vital in understanding how
relationships work: they are not one-sided and both par-
ticipants need to gain something otherwise the relationship will stagnate or disintegrate.

## Who are you?

There are many facets to your personality that make up
you, which is why you are unique; no one else has exactly
the same match with all the different combinations of likes
and dislikes and personality traits. Consider the following
questions and write down your answers. As well as helping
you to understand yourself, some of the information you
note can form the basis of early conversations with people
you meet.

- What do you do for a living? How do you spend your
  free time? What things do you avoid altogether or put
  off to the last moment?
- What things did you enjoy in school? What things did
  you dislike? What things were good about your
  upbringing? What things were bad?

- What animals, foods, clothes, colours, plants, books, music, films do you like and dislike?
- How would you spend an ideal day or evening? Where would you like to go on holiday? Where have you been on holiday?
- What things frighten you or make you laugh?
- Whom do you most like and most dislike to be with? Why?
- What values and beliefs do you hold? What do you want out of life, what are your ambitions and dreams?

Part of who you are is to do with your personality and your answers to the questions below may indicate whether you need to try to address underlying problems with the way you react to things or feel about things, as these can hamper your relationships.

*What are your negative qualities?* Do you easily get angry or violent? Are you insensitive, impatient, rude or aggressive?

*What are your positive qualities?* Are you considerate, kind, caring, funny or energetic?

*How do you react to negative life events?* Do you completely break down and become unable to cope or do you rise to the challenge and never give up until you're through the worst? Do you seek help or do you bottle up your problems? Do you lash out when things go wrong? Do you try to see the positive side to everything?

*How do you react to positive life events?* For example, when a friend tells you she is going to get married, do you under-react and give a few tepid words of congratulation; or do you go over the top and immediately drag her into a bar to celebrate? Do you jump and shout and scream when you've achieved something major or do you quietly tell your closest friend?

*What qualities do you look for in a friend?* Some suggestions are: being kind, caring, understanding, loyal, trustworthy, honest and sympathetic; accepting personal faults; having a good sense of humour; being someone to be silly and have fun with; being able to keep secrets and not gossip.

*What qualities do you look for in a life partner?* Many of these will probably be the same as for a friend, but there may be additions such as: being affectionate, faithful and non-violent; being a caring and considerate sexual partner; not embarrassing you in front of others or making you feel small; having a love of children (if you want children or already have them); being able to communicate feelings and talk problems through in an open way, and allowing you to have a life of your own without controlling you.

*What qualities have you to offer?* If you expect certain qualities in others, it is only fair that you are able, or strive, to offer the same qualities. Some suggestions not already used are:

- I am a good listener.
- I take responsibility for the things I say and do.
- I do not always expect others to be able to do the things I can do: I understand we are all different and have different strengths and weaknesses.
- I am understanding of my, and others', failings.
- I know my limitations and do not pretend to be something I am not.
- I understand how my past affects my current relationships and am wary of repeating damaging influences with others.
- I am aware of shutting people out when they have hurt me so try to explain why I feel the way I do and why I have acted in such a way when I want the relationship to survive.
- I am able to say sorry when I have made a mistake or have unintentionally hurt someone.
- I am sensitive to other cultures, religions and social classes and do not purport to be 'favoured' or superior, or inferior, to others because of these differences.

- I can communicate my thoughts and feelings well and am prepared to disclose at appropriate levels.
- I am very sensitive to others in emotional pain and can comfort them with words and by physical touch.
- I know the importance of keeping confidences.
- I can read others' body language and facial expressions so understand the complete picture of what they are trying to say and so I can respond appropriately.
- I try to be non-judgmental in my dealings with others but know on which areas I fail to do this and why, and so know when to keep quiet to avoid conflict.
- I try to avoid conflict by finding something on which to compromise.
- I try to accept others as they are without trying to change them or feeling the need to.
- I stick up for others and myself when I think something unjustified has been done or said.
- I am aware when I feel my anger getting out of control so I can take steps to avoid a painful confrontation before I say or do things I know I will later regret.

*What qualities would you like to offer that you don't already have?* For example: patience and tolerance. What could you do to try to achieve these? A suggestion might be to remind yourself that not everyone works at your speed and that they may need more time, or that they may not feel their time is as pressed as yours.

*How good a friend are you?* Are you prepared to listen when your friends have something to tell? Are you able to offer what your friends need when they are in trouble? For example: practical guidance or advice, practical help, sympathy, comfort, continued support rather than a one-off effort, confidence-boosting words to make them feel better about themselves, reassurance, understanding, non-judgmental comments and respect.

*How do you think others see you?* Think about the things people have told you and the messages you have received from the way they behave towards you. For example, if they think you are miserable, they will keep telling you to cheer up; if they think you are boring, they will yawn in your presence and not pay attention to what you have to say. Try to create a column of positive things people think about you and a column of negative things people think about you. Then ask yourself what you can do to make people see you in a more positive light. For example, if they think you are selfish, what can you do to change your behaviour to show that you are not selfish? This does not mean turning yourself into a doormat, but occasionally putting your needs aside when you see that someone else is in genuine difficulty.

### Personal confidence

It is extremely hard to start new relationships when you have zero, or close to zero, personal confidence. Having a lack of confidence prevents you from approaching another person and initiating conversation, or giving full and relaxed responses to someone who approaches you, as you may believe this person could not possibly be interested in what you might have to say. Yet people do not have deep and involved conversations on their first meeting: they talk about neutral subjects such as their surroundings, the weather and the number of trains that get cancelled on the line on which they travel; you don't have to say anything scintillating.

So, before you can improve your skills when dealing with other people (and this in itself will give you confidence) you first need to change your attitude about yourself.

*Liking yourself.* Go back to the list you made about the personal qualities you'd like to offer but don't already have. Put an asterisk against things you can change and write down how you can change them. Then you can work at changing yourself so that you become more likeable to yourself and other people. Try to accept the things you genuinely can't change: they are a part of you.

*Loving yourself.* Loving is being very sure that you are a great person and accepting yourself entirely, including your faults. You know that you are not useless or unworthy because of some minor faults or even a major one if the reason for it is understandable under the circumstances. When loving yourself, you see yourself as a whole person who has done the best with your personality and the pitfalls of life that have come your way.

*Increasing your personal confidence.* Keeping fit helps you to feel confident about yourself and your body. When you feel good you are more likely to be receptive to others and be pleased to socialise with them. Also, it will help you keep an erect posture as your muscles will be strengthened. If you look confident, you will feel confident and others will believe you are confident, whether or not this is the case.

Get used to socialising with others and chatting to complete strangers: it will feel natural with practice.

A good starting place is talking to others in queues, in waiting rooms, at bus stops, at parties and so on – where you can easily talk to someone without it necessarily leading to anything else (such as a business or romantic relationship) so that it is pressure free. You could make a comment on something you have both just seen or on the lateness of the bus. Or you could ask a question such as, 'Have I missed the 5.15 train to . . .?' or, 'Would you mind saving my seat for me while I go to the toilet?' or, 'How long have you been waiting? Are you next?' or, 'Could you tell me the time, please?' or, 'Do you have change for . . .?'

*Increasing your self-esteem.* Try to smooth out the dips in your self-esteem by reminding yourself at vulnerable moments of all the positive qualities you have. Remind yourself of the people who love you or have affection for you and those who enjoy your company. Remind yourself of the times you have been proud of yourself for having achieved something that was hard for you.

One enormous way of boosting your self-esteem is in improving the relationships you have and in making new ones. Friendships can be wonderful for improving your mental health and are one of the most rewarding things in the world when they go right: think of the ultimate friendship as falling in love with someone and having that love returned. If this has happened to you, you know how wonderful and good about yourself that makes you feel.

### Friends and friendships

Friends are people you like, care about and respect, and are usually not part of your family – although partners can be good friends, the relationship is different and has more to bind the two people together than an ordinary friendship.

Friends are people with whom you have something in common including: temperament – you might both be party animals or desperately shy, for example; being a parent; enjoying going to discos; working at the same place; being from the same minority group or sharing similar life experiences. And they are people to do things with such as play sport, go shopping or see a film. Having things in common and doing things with a friend binds you together to give you a sense of belonging, which is important because you can both talk about the things that interest you without risk of boring the other person.

As well as it being risky to rely heavily on one person (in case something should happen to upset the balance of the relationship and it fails, or if the person leaves the area or dies, for example), one friend should not be expected to fulfil all your needs. You may need several people to fulfil all of them, as each person will have different strengths and weaknesses, just like you will fulfil a different need in each of your friends. In doing this, you complement one another and fit like jigsaw pieces. For example, one of your friends may be great fun to be with and will fulfil your need to have a good time. Another may be a good listener and will fulfil your need to share your burdens with a sympathetic person. A third may be practical and serious and may be helpful in finding solutions over problems you might have.

As well as different friends fulfilling different needs, your friendships will have a varying level of intimacy: some you may barely know at all but maintain the relationship for convenience such as having children the same age who play together, or needing someone with whom to play squash or have lunch when you are at work. All of these relationships fit into your life like a jigsaw; some pieces are larger than others and you spend more time with those people. The smaller pieces keep your world ticking over and complete the puzzle, making you feel whole and satisfied.

Of course, not everyone is in the happy position of having his jigsaw puzzle complete. By following the advice and information in this book you can change your smaller jigsaw pieces into bigger ones, and find some new pieces, big and small. It may be that you will never have a complete puzzle because you or your partner regularly has to move from one area to another through work; but if you are continually on the lookout for new opportunities to speak to people and are open to new relationships it will certainly help to fill any gaps that have become available.

*Friendships and self-esteem.* Generally, people have friends at the same educational level and from comparable backgrounds because they feel more comfortable with others who are similar to themselves. For example, if you are extremely slow at picking up new skills, did not do well at school and feel useless at sports, you are likely to feel uncomfortable if you spend a great deal of time with people who have been academically successful, are in high powered jobs and are very competitive in sports. Spending much time with people to whom you feel you are subordinate can lower your self-esteem and make you dissatisfied with your lot.

However, this does not mean you should be deliberately narrow in your choice of friends, discounting people because they don't fit your rigid criteria. If you enjoy a person's company and he makes you feel good, he can make an excellent friend and any background differences may be unimportant.

### Friendship rules

*Give support* by commiserating with your friend when things go wrong and listening to him when he has something to confide. Be understanding and sympathetic.

*Give help* in times of need. This can be either practical or informational help, or emotional support.

*Show care* by asking after your friend's health, reassuring her when she has doubts, giving feedback on how you feel about her and what things you like about her, and show affection. In men, this could be by teasing or patting your friend's shoulder. In women, it could be by kissing and hugging on meeting.

*Show respect* by accepting that your friend is an individual and does not have to be exactly like you, and by being non-judgmental.

*Be loyal* by sticking up for your friend in his absence.

*Be faithful* by remaining that person's friend all the time – not just when it suits you. This also means you can be relied upon in times of need.

*Share your life* by talking about things that are important to you, by saying how you feel about things, by celebrating successes, having fun and doing things together.

Things you must not do are:

- Show jealousy if your friend spends time with other friends or gets a partner.
- Embarrass your friend in public.
- Gossip about your friend.
- Tell others about your friend's confidences.
- Lie.
- Steal.
- Sleep with your friend's partner.

# 2

# MAKING NEW FRIENDS

There are opportunities to make new friends at every social occasion and every time you interact with someone new at work or on your travels. Understanding the process of making friends will help you recognise how you are doing and whether the relationship has potential so that you know when to let go and when to follow through to focus on receptive people for a surer outcome of friendship.

### The process of making a new friend
How you and another person perceive, and relate to, each other from the moment you meet is determined by what is said and the way it is said, and can make the difference between success and failure.

*First impressions* are the most important in a relationship, as very often people don't get a second chance if they get it wrong. Positive impressions are gained by noting areas of commonality such as having gone to the same school or university, both of you having children or both of you showing appreciation of your surroundings. Negative impressions could be given by behaving or dressing very differently from the other person, or stating opposing views, setting up subconscious barriers between you. Or you might find out that the other person lives her life contrary to how you feel people ought to live their lives, increasing the emotional distance between you. You can then very quickly decide you don't like her at all.

It may be that you are extremely careful with your money and have just heard her say how much her outfit cost or you may have never been able to afford a foreign holiday and she is describing her second extravagant holiday abroad that year. Or she may be boasting about how she rang in sick the other day because she wanted to go shopping with her mother and you have never done a dishonest thing in your life.

Whatever information you get in the first few minutes determines whether you want to get to know the other person better or get away as soon as you can. It may be that a first negative impression has been wrong but you may not linger long enough to find out. You can get false positive impressions too. The person you thought of as really caring because you saw how he behaved towards his partner, for example, might turn out to be someone who puts on a show of being nice in public but is actually a bully in the home. Whatever the impression and whether true or false, it takes a long time to change: first impressions stick.

So, unless you want to make some sort of statement and are prepared to live with the consequences, conform to the dress code everyone else has adopted, moderate extremes of behaviour and don't be too ready to spout opinions. And try not to be in too much of a rush to write off the person you are talking to as non-friendship material. People often don't show their true selves, especially if they are under pressure or feel anxious about socialising.

Bear in mind that friendship does not only fail from a person's genuine lack of interest in getting to know you. He can also pretend a lack of interest out of fear of rejection, or he may handle the conversation badly because he has poor social skills. It is up to you to try to work out what the reason is – if you care enough to talk to him for that long.

*Subsequent impressions* from arranging to meet up regularly, or from meeting by chance, give you the opportunity gradually to get to know the other person by giving a little – and only a little – of yourself away each time. Providing information about yourself in small, cautious amounts allows you to see what effect it has on the other person and to establish whether you can trust her with more important personal data.

If these meetings go well, you may succeed in moving on to an established close relationship. If they don't, you can end up with relationship failure where you don't try to see the other person again – or have a stagnant relationship where conversations remain on a superficial level. Some people are afraid to become more intimate because they worry about being hurt or betrayed, and so don't reap the rewards of having strong and enduring friendships. If this is you, try to move forward, albeit very slowly, with someone you trust or you could be very lonely.

*Established relationships* can be extremely rewarding. However, you have to make an effort to keep them going, showing interest in the other person and being prepared to give as well as take. You should mark important events by at least saying, for example, happy birthday or happy anniversary. Some people like to give cards and small gifts for birthdays or the birth of a baby. Remember sad times too, and check that your friend is all right, for example, on the anniversary of his wife's death.

A good level of intimacy is expected with established relationships so you have to be prepared to divulge a great deal about yourself and listen to a comparable amount about the other person, since emotional commitments need to be balanced.

Serious flouting of friendship rules (see Chapter 1) can lead to an abrupt end in the relationship: lesser rule breaking may halt the progression to an extremely close relationship unless trust can be re-established. Problems may arise, however, if you are dealing with someone who has a far greater number of rules than you or will not accept any kind of failure to stick to them. If you are like this and wonder why you don't have sufficient friends, perhaps you should rewrite some of those rules and become more relaxed in your approach to friendship.

### Disclosure

Disclosure is telling people about yourself and defining yourself – letting people know who you are through what you choose to tell them. Disclosure also helps you and the people you meet find out whether you have things in common – the more you have in common, the closer you are likely to become. When you disclose, you also get to know yourself better as you consider what personal information to divulge and how you feel about the people you talk to. When other people disclose, it gives them the opportunity to tell you about themselves, how they feel about you and whether they agree or disagree with what you say, which helps build rapport.

*Appropriateness* of disclosures is vital. If you disclose everything about yourself at the first or second meeting, you could put the other person off, plus you are unlikely to have your disclosures valued – she could well pass on what you have said to other people. Think about levels of disclosure being like the layers in an onion – you give a little of yourself away over time starting with the uppermost layers first that represent the most superficial information about yourself. Low-risk disclosures unlikely to damage your reputation include telling someone your name, your age, whereabouts you live and work and whether you have a family of your own. It won't much matter if the person reveals this information to others as it is generally known.

Only when you have covered the superficial information

should you, on subsequent meetings, delve deeper into your life and reveal the inner you. The other person should match any lower layer disclosures you make, although not necessarily straightaway. If he doesn't, you should halt the progression of your deeper level disclosures until there is a commitment from him to allow you to get to know him better.

The level to which you, and the other person, are prepared to confide, determines how close you become. Intimacy will only be achieved when both sides disclose high-risk information and each side is confident that the disclosures will be kept secret: if confidence has been broken, the person who confided is unlikely to confide again; or at least not for a long time, after trust has been rebuilt.

*Timing* your disclosures is also important. For example, it is inappropriate to disclose to your lover for the first time that you love her when she is already late for a train and cannot give time to reply or give you the level of attention you might hope for after making such a caring declaration.

*Understanding the environment you are in* allows you to adapt your behaviour and be careful about your disclosures. For example, although it would be inappropriate to talk about your haemorrhoids at a dinner party, it would be very appropriate in a doctor's consulting room.

Sometimes it is appropriate to make deep disclosures on short acquaintance. For example, if you are talking to a therapist, you gain nothing by trying to hide what is going on in your life – in any case, he is bound by strict rules of confidentiality. The same applies to the confessional box of the Roman Catholic faith. When travelling, you might disclose highly because the anonymity recreates the security experienced in a consulting room: you are on a fixed journey with a complete stranger whom you are unlikely ever to meet again and who is unlikely to meet any of your acquaintances, so it may not matter if you are not discreet; there is virtually no risk of anyone else ever finding out about your conversation.

## Gender differences with disclosure
Although generalisations cannot be applied to individuals, it is more likely that men have problems disclosing, particularly their feelings and vulnerabilities: they may feel they have to put on a macho front to be accepted as a man. Some men may worry they might be considered homosexual if they show the softer side of themselves. However, heterosexual relationships can fail if the man cannot be open with his feelings as it is harder to clear up misunderstandings and to reach an intimacy his female partner may crave.

A lack of ability to disclose in men, thereby cutting themselves off from emotional support, is thought to be a contributory factor in male suicides, which are greater than female suicides in the UK. If you are a man and have chosen your confidante well, you will be admired rather than ridiculed for showing a vulnerable side.

## Cultural differences with disclosure
People from Western societies are more likely to disclose things to others – or to disclose more readily when the time is right – than those from other cultures if the subject is taboo or disapproved of. For example, an unmarried woman in her late twenties from Western society would probably not think twice about telling someone about her lover but in a culture where such a woman is considered unclean and wicked she is not likely to dare speak of it.

## Risks of disclosure
By letting others get to know you, you may worry about the consequences. Will they ever want to speak to you

again? Will they consider you have 'low-status' and not want to be seen out with you? Will they misunderstand what you wanted to say? Will they respect your confidences or will they tell other people? Will they think you pathetic, daft or insane if you tell them about your problems? This is why new friendships should be taken slowly so that you can judge when to say certain things; it can be hard to get it right.

There is also the risk of someone liking you too much after having shown your vulnerabilities, falling in love when one of you – or both of you – is not 'free' to start a romantic or sexual relationship.

### Communication in friendships

There are four ways in which you communicate with other people: by talking, listening, touching and looking. For real communication to occur, they need to be shared by both parties. How well do you communicate?

*Talking and listening.* You can do all the talking while the other person listens, or pretends to listen. But if the listening person makes no sound at all (such as not saying, 'Really?' or, 'I didn't know that' or, 'I am sorry' or, 'Oh, dear') then your words may as well fall on deaf ears, there being no true communication at all: you are talking *at* the other person.

Remaining aloof and uninvolved tells you that the other person is uninterested and has no wish to get to know you better. Poor listening prevents intimacy as the conversation is one-sided: the listener doesn't divulge how he feels about what you've said and doesn't contribute a similar experience of his own. (Also see Chapter 7.)

*Looking and touching.* If you are interested in the other person and in what she has to say, you look at her a great deal. If she doesn't look at you back, it shows a lack of interest. If you touch her but there is no responding touch back at an appropriate point, it shows that she does not want to become intimate, discouraging you from touching her again.

### Social networks

Friendships form a social network. Some people have large social networks with many members; others have small ones with fewer members. The social support that you get from your network is not dependent on the number of members it contains but on the level of intimacy between its members. For example, one person could have a very large social network with twenty members who are seen regularly at group functions like parties or in the office while a second person has a social network of three intimate friends. The second person could get more social support than the first because there is little intimacy in casual friendships in large group environments.

*A loose social network* has much variation among its members in categories of things like career, social status, political views, income, and religion, and more room for nonconformity, such as in dress or way of living, and more opportunities for new members to join. However, it is also easier to lose members, as the ties between them are not as close-knit as they are with cliques (see below). The other drawback is that if a member is in trouble the response time for help is greater than with cliques since members may not meet often, or at all if they are unconnected with other members, and so won't share information promptly. But because there is such a variety among members, if someone needs informational help, loose networks are more useful as there is more chance that someone in your social network knows someone else who can help.

*A clique* is a group of people who are closely knitted together, usually having much in common, and all social-ising with each other on a very regular or frequent basis. If the clique is work-related, members may socialise with non-members when away from work, making it a weaker clique than one where members socialise both in and out of work.

Cliques can have their own special rules and if members don't conform to the rules, they may be rejected. This puts pressure on members and some may not be able to live up to the expectations of the group. If, for example, you belong to a fundamental Christian clique, you might be required to live a blameless life, to spread the word of Jesus, to convert people not only to Christianity but to that particular brand of Christianity and, if you fail in one of these, you might be shunned by other group members. Having friends from only one clique is risky: if you get rejected because of breaking a group rule, all members will probably reject you, depriving you of friends and social support which can leave you feeling lonely and low.

It is harder for new members to join cliques: members may feel satisfied with their level of social contact and so may not actively seek new friendships. If you arrive in a small community, for example, there would be no reason for existing members of the clique to invite you to join them, or if they did, you would be expected to adhere to the group's expectations and any deviation from this would be unlikely to be tolerated. Also, clique members will know each other so well that they may not want the effort of starting afresh with another member and, even if you were allowed to join them, it would be a long time before you had the same status as the other members. The hundreds of little confidences shared by the long-standing members may also exclude you from much of their talk, or you may find that the group goes silent as you approach since the others are sharing things unknown to you, or are even talking about you behind your back.

It is also harder for existing members to leave a clique: if one member appears to stray, the other members may seek her out to find out what is wrong and take steps to try to keep her within the group. You might see this as positive if they do this in a supportive light, but negative if they want to keep you imprisoned in a religious sect, for example. Another downside of cliques is that if you want to form a closer relationship with one member of the clique, it is less likely your confidences will be kept. The temptation to share them with other group members may be too much. Or your extra intimacy with this person may not last and so allegiance may be easily switched. Because of this, there is an advantage in having friends outside a clique with whom to confide.

If a clique member is in trouble, the response time for help is very quick as members are close to hand and pull together as a group, but cliques are not so good in providing informational help as they are not sufficiently diverse.

*Isolated friends* who don't socialise with anyone else in your social network can be very valuable: you can choose the level of intimacy you have secure in the knowledge that even if they do tell someone else, they won't be telling anyone you know. If you have several isolated friends you can get varied support from them without any of them knowing the complete picture about what is going on in your life. This is good if you find it hard to trust people: you can confide part of a problem to one person, and another part to another. It is also good to spread around your confidences if you have been badly betrayed in the past: you can then confide with more security without cutting yourself off from all social support.

It is also good to have isolated friends when you have problems very close to home such as with your partner or a fellow clique member and secrecy needs to be assured.

Opposite you can see a diagram showing my social network. Friends A to G are from school and university whom I rarely see because of distances involved and family commitments; I sce them separately and they don't socialise with each other. J and H were friends at work and

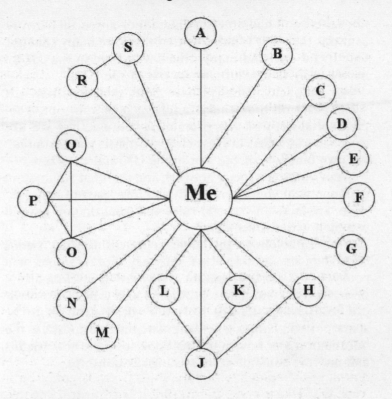

when I joined the same school to teach we became mutual friends and I married J.

Then I moved area with J and made friends with two of the people he works with: K and L. O, P, Q and Me form a clique as we are mutual friends with children: we live in the grounds of the college, with about 40 others, where our husbands work. I got to know R and S and became friendly with them through my work as a houseparent, but they don't live in the college. M and N are two completely independent friends who have nothing to do with the college, where I was educated or where I've worked.

Social networks are not always static. For example, a

few years ago I had drawn a diagram of my social network as it was then and I find now that there are many changes. One friend died and many others who lived in the college moved away to new jobs, many out of the UK.

For simplicity, families have been excluded from my social network. Sometimes family members in some people's social network are prominent because they are like close friends, others are less close with little social contact: my own family is spread out in the UK and elsewhere.

Draw your own social network and see what you have in common with your friends. Do you form part of a clique? If so, are there any special rules and what do you have in common with its members?

Assign a colour to the circles representing your friends depending on your level of intimacy. For example, you could choose red to represent a very intimate relationship, orange a fairly intimate relationship and yellow, a superficial relationship. If you feel your social network to be sparse, or you have too few intimate relationships, use the information and advice in this book to make new friends and improve some of your existing relationships.

# 3

# THINGS THAT PREVENT INTIMACY

Intimate relationships have high levels of disclosure, trust and loyalty and are very satisfying, but many people find it difficult getting to the intimate stage because of various factors that interfere with the progression of their relationships.

### Changeable things that interfere with making friends
Try not to see these problems as insurmountable, rather a challenge to be met. Are you content to let things be or do you want more for yourself? It's up to you.

### Out-of-date rules
You may have been given rules as a child that you have accepted as lifelong rules without questioning their continuing validity or usefulness. Some rules you may have unconsciously given yourself such as for a man to think he must never talk to a woman because she may misunderstand him and think he is chatting her up. Write your rules down and address each one in turn to stop them from unnecessarily blocking your relationships. Ask yourself: Is it a sensible rule? Is it out-of-date? How can I adapt the rule to suit my needs today?

As a woman, you may have been given the rule: I must never speak to strangers. But it is not a sensible rule. If you never talk to strangers, you would never meet anyone new. If you are in a crowded place among many people, it does not matter if you exchange a few words with a stranger; it's what makes the day enjoyable, communicating with those around you and sharing the moment. It is also an out-of-date rule: you are no longer a child and can see the difference between unsafe lonely places and safe busy places. You can adapt your rule to: I must not draw attention to myself in a lonely place by talking to anyone else or by approaching them as it might not be safe.

As a man, you may have been given the rule: I should always open the door to a lady and let her go in first.

This is not a sensible rule if it is followed on every occasion: if a woman were already in front of you, she'd be surprised and irritated if you elbowed her out of the way just to do the honours of opening the door for her. On a romantic date, it would be very appropriate for you to be attentive but in a work environment you'd be ridiculed hurrying to get to a door first just so that you could open it for a woman. It is also out-of-date: nowadays men talk about women, not ladies. You can adapt your rule to: I should open doors for women as a matter of courtesy when I feel it appropriate.

**Fearing betrayal**
Fear of having your trust betrayed because it has been in the past will make you want to limit intimacy rather than pursue it, scared of making yourself vulnerable in the future. However, after a recovery period you may feel that you are prepared tentatively to try reaching similar levels of intimacy again with someone else: if you feel that you are unable to trust anyone, consider having counselling to resolve underlying problems. Otherwise, build up new relationships very slowly by spending only small amounts

of time with people at first and by being careful with what you divulge: over a period of several years you could achieve intimacy.

With existing relationships, choose isolated friends to test whether they can be trusted with snippets of information: you don't have to give any two friends the same information if you feel unsafe so that no one will have the complete picture of you. However, over time, you might decide to move one relationship further than another, gradually disclosing more and more.

### Fear of getting hurt

Being afraid of getting hurt will make you wary of becoming close to someone as, for example, the pain of parting from bereavement or the person moving away is so great. However, it is your friendships that sustain you through troubled times. It helps if you have several friends so that you don't rely heavily on one: you should increase your social network rather than decrease it.

### Having a heavy accent

Having a heavy regional or non-indigenous accent that people can't understand prevents communication and can leave you open to ridicule. Being the only one to have a posh accent also makes you stand out from the crowd and you may fear ridicule and not being accepted into friendship groups. Try to dilute a heavy accent of any kind to fit in with the people around you so that the physical barrier of not being able to understand, and the emotional barrier of knowing that you come from vastly different backgrounds, are lowered.

### Poor social skills

Having poor social skills prevents communication and understanding. For example, if another person behaves as though she does not enjoy your company you are less likely to enjoy hers and it will show through your behaviour that you don't like her; so both of you will be less likely to take the relationship further even though you may have initially misread the situation. By learning how to behave socially, you will overcome your own social inadequacies and be more tolerant of others'.

## Social anxiety

Being socially anxious inhibits confident and fluent social behaviour. Socially anxious people behave timidly in society fearing critical evaluation, withdrawing from the risks involved – such as rejection or ridicule – and are too afraid to voice their true feelings, hiding behind a mask of indifference. They prevent others getting to know and love them, cutting themselves off from positive social support, feeling too ashamed of their inadequacies to let others close.

The exact picture of social anxiety, and its most extreme form of social phobia, is different for each person: no two people necessarily have the same match of stressors. Also, many people with social anxiety have good social skills and can perform well with people they are close to, in environments where they feel comfortable. But outside this comfort zone, stress interferes with their developing intimate relationships. By honing and frequently practising your social skills with other people, you can become more confident and more at ease in previously stressful situations.

## Inability to disclose

As mentioned in Chapter 2, men tend to have more difficulty than women in reaching high levels of intimacy in a friendship because they are unable to reveal how they feel about things or let people get close. However, either sex can have trouble achieving intimacy through disclosure. If you find it hard, start with small low-risk disclosures and gradually work up to bigger ones with people you trust.

**Personality**

Some personalities, if in evidence, are a direct turn-off to achieving intimacy whether in a work or leisure situation. There are, of course, times when you deliberately behave in certain ways in response to something done to you or that has happened. However, the personalities described below assume that this is how the person is most of the time with most people. The ideal, assertive, personality is described last.

*If you are arrogant,* you are of the opinion that you are always right and know more than the incompetent people around you. You won't respect other people easily and they won't respect you as they see you as someone who only thinks of yourself – and thinks rather too much of yourself. They will not be tempted to disclose to you as they will not trust you with their vulnerabilities, fearing that you won't understand them or value the confidences they make.

*If you are quick tempered* and fiery, others may consider you a walking emotional time bomb waiting to explode in someone else's face. It will make people avoid you and be wary of all future social interactions with you.

*If you are patronising,* you don't treat other people as your equal. People won't warm to you as they may fear you will make fun of them for being foolish or because of a vulnerability they have revealed.

*If you are superior,* you are likely to put others down at every opportunity to make you look more able and efficient. This is likely to instil dislike and resentment of you. Other people will wonder why you have such a high opinion of yourself, watching for the first sign of weakness. They will not trust you with their confidences. Having a superior role, as in being a boss to an employee or a therapist to a client or a doctor to a patient, involves showing trust, care and concern if the role is not to be abused.

*If you are very passive* you will be known to be too afraid to venture an opinion and too unsure and insecure to manage your own life without constant reassurance. This does not command respect so you would be unlikely to be someone others go to in times of trouble. People may socialise with you because you make them feel comfortable, agreeing with them and allowing them to dictate how you spend your time; or they may enjoy taking advantage of you. But your friendships are not likely to be equal or deep. This might not hold for being friends with another person who is also very passive: she might only want to confide in someone who has a similar personality, as she might feel threatened by more assertive people.

*If you are distant*, you do not invite confidences of any kind as you never let anyone get close enough to want to unburden himself to you and you never give confidences of your own. There is an emotional barrier between you and other people that others can detect, but they have no reason to try to break through this barrier as they see you as indifferent and unwilling to make an effort towards friendship.

*If you are assertive*, you can still have elements of passivity – such as when you choose to use caring skills, and aggression – such as when you need to show someone you are angry. But you are socially skilful and can judge when to be caring or angry and know how to behave in between the extremes to show respect for others and yourself. You behave in a rewarding way to others who seek you out, are loyal to your friends, honouring confidences and are willing to help. You understand that relationships are two-way things that require work to reap the pleasures. Although this is the ideal, and it may not be possible for everyone to achieve all the time, it gives a goal to work towards. It is possible to change the way you interact with others and the advice in the rest of the book will help you reach your personal goal.

**Loneliness**
Lonely behaviour does not invite attention or social contact, increasing your isolation. It includes not smiling, not making eye contact, being self-absorbed, being unresponsive and negative when interacting with strangers, and not attending to personal care, looking unkempt and unclean. Lonely men are more likely to act aggressively or hostilely towards strangers than lonely women and non-lonely people: aggression drives people away so this behaviour won't improve the situation.

Being very inflexible in expectations of friendship will also make you lonely. For example, believing that someone is a good friend until she has made a minor mistake and then never forgiving her for it dooms the relationship. Instead, why not talk about it, try to understand why the mistake happened and fight to rescue the relationship? Most of us make minor errors in friendship – by repairing the friendship you can make it stronger.

If you are lonely you may have very low self-esteem, believing you are worthless and unlovable. You may feel isolated, miserable and depressed; bitter and angry; feel you are on the outside looking in, and embarrassed that others might guess how unhappy your life is. You might find it hard to trust people, expecting to be made fun of, and might not know how to cooperate with others or talk to them as an equal. If the situation is not reversed, you might feel suicidal. It is more likely that lonely people over-eat, over-sleep, cry, watch television in excess, drink alcohol in excess and take tranquillisers. If this applies to you, ask your doctor to be referred for counselling, and work hard at improving your relationships.

**Your past**
The older you get, the more emotional baggage you have that interferes with developing relationships. Bad feelings that have built up from the past can stay and haunt you

making you feel, for example, utterly worthless. If you have trouble overcoming past experiences seek professional help: your past cannot be changed but the way you view it might.

## Relationship messages

Messages you have picked up through experiences with other people, either by you being directly involved or by you seeing how someone else deals with a problem, can affect your relationships. These messages can include whether to show or hide feelings, how to behave when you meet people and how to solve arguments.

The things that are most important to the people around you might become the things that are most important to you: if they value something, the chances are you will. If they scorn something, you probably will too. And in seeing how people around you value their relationships gives you ideas on the value you should put upon yours. For example, if you saw your father regularly treating your mother in an abusive manner, you may have trouble valuing your own partner.

These things don't hold true every time with everyone: but if you are aware of how your upbringing and the people around you have influenced you, you can start to think about what is genuinely you. It is possible to make decisions to change the way you behave towards others.

Here are some suggestions of relationship messages from other people:

- You were left alone for much of your childhood: 'You must seek your own entertainment' or, 'You are not worth talking to' or, 'You are not fun to be with.' These messages will make you feel bad about yourself.
- Your parents argued a great deal and threw things at each other: 'You solve arguments by shouting, by getting violent and by not listening to the other person.' This message tells you to react to things in a confrontational way and that you have to go all out to win.

- Your parents never asked why you did something wrong, they just punished you for it: 'Obedience is more important than understanding between people' or, 'You must never question your parents: you must do what they tell you or suffer the consequences.' These messages could be extended to any authority figure and you may have trouble standing up for yourself or making your needs known. It also tells you that your emotional needs are unimportant, and that relationships are functional: not for give and take or for showing concern.

- Your parents always sat down together to talk problems through and to find a middle ground that was acceptable to both: 'Cooperation is important and it can solve problems.' This is a positive message that shows a useful technique for avoiding conflict.

- Your parents never had friends drop in on them. Nor did they casually visit others: 'Friends are people you make appointments with' or, 'Friends should only come when it's convenient.' This gives a very formal view of friendships that many people would not find helpful. Friends should be understanding of an untidy house, should not be in competition with each other and should be comfortable enough with each other to call in when they are close by.

- Your parents treated your brother more leniently than you (you are female): 'You are less worthy than your brother' or, 'You are more wayward or we trust you less than we do your brother, so you have to be dealt with more harshly.' This is likely to give you feelings of inferiority to your brother and perhaps to men in general. You can clearly see that men are treated differently from women.

- You were bullied at school: 'You are worthless and spineless because you can't stand up for yourself.' This is likely to give you very low self-esteem and you may be frightened of meeting new people believing that they will somehow guess your humiliation and laugh at you. Or you may feel that wherever you go someone will be there to take advantage of you. By learning how to be assertive you will avoid 'victim' body language and behaviour, and people will not see you as an adult target to bully (see Chapters 8 and 10).

Here are two suggestions of relationship messages you can get from adverts:

- A tissue advert showing women comforting a crying friend: 'Women should comfort friends when they are upset.' This might tell you that you are inadequate as a friend if you can't show sympathy for someone in distress. Or it might show you what good friends do, helping you become a more caring friend.

- A car advert showing a couple splitting up where one takes the car and smiles because she's ended up with what's most important: 'Don't stay and try to sort out your differences. Get what you can and leave as fast as possible.' This tells you not to work at relationships, particularly romantic ones, and that material things are more important than friendships.

Books you read, films you see, famous people you hear about, and observing or hearing about complete strangers can also influence your relationships. Watch for negative as well as positive influences: it is far easier to spot other people making mistakes than spot your own as you don't look upon yourself objectively. If a relationship message you've been given is unhelpful, discard it and replace it with one of your own.

### Non-changeable things that interfere with making friends

The possibility of having others see you in what you perceive to be a negative light can prevent your relationships from developing past the first tentative and superficial stage.

Although you cannot change stark reality, you can change your attitude towards it and the expectations you have of others so that these things don't remain permanent blocks: you might be able to face a trusted friend knowing about them even though you cannot change the original problem.

### Being embarrassed about a family member
Eccentricity or a drug, alcohol or mental health problem in a relative who lives with you, may make you reluctant to bring anyone home, fearing that others won't accept you or your family if they were to know the secret you try so carefully to hide. Or your partner may be unpredictably violent and abusive and you fear an eruption in front of witnesses.

### Having a health or mental health problem
Having any health problem of which you are ashamed can make you ensure that others don't find out, fearing their negative judgment of you. This prevents others getting close to you; there may be regular periods when you have to hide yourself away while the illness is evident which makes you very unavailable and people will interpret this as you being uninterested in them.

### Having a very different educational background
Being poorly educated can make you feel inferior among people who are better educated – fearing rejection and ridicule. Having a superior education to people around you can make you choose to avoid them, either because you don't want to go 'downmarket' or because you believe they will not accept you in their friendship group.

### Living in poor conditions
Having an undesirable place to live and having very little money can make you fear others seeing how financially stretched you are. You might not want others to see that

your home is a council owned property or that you live in a tower block when they live in plush houses and you might be ashamed of the area in which you live. You might not want them to see your threadbare carpet or find out that your electricity keeps getting cut off because there isn't enough money to pay the bills. If a group of people you know is going out somewhere you might regularly decline to join them because you have no money but are too proud to admit the truth: they will perceive you as distant and uninterested.

**Having a chaperone**
Always having someone with you when you are out of the house stifles intimacy and can make you and any companion very self-conscious about what you say and do. Also, you may not be free to pick with whom you spend time; it might be decided for you by your parents or guardians.

**Being from an ethnic or religious minority**
Being from a minority group can make you very self-conscious, especially if you dress very differently from those around you. You may not expect anyone from the majority or host culture to want to know you, or you may have had so many experiences of racially motivated attacks that you avoid anyone from other cultures as a matter of course, discouraging overtures of friendship, fearing having your customs and traditions scorned.

**Other things that prevent intimacy**
Being tied by a busy work schedule or having to look after children, a sick partner or an elderly parent makes it hard to keep friends or build new friendships. However, you can perhaps reorganise work to make time, and find other people tied to the home who you can meet up with for support.

Friendships can be damaged by your behaviour: sleeping with your friend's partner or breaking an important confidence, being so affected by alcoholism and drug misuse that you behave very inappropriately and refuse to get help, or through other more minor behavioural lapses that might be forgiven but serve to distance you from your friend. Your relationship can also be damaged by your friend's behaviour: doing similar things already mentioned.

Any of the following life events can also reduce or prevent intimacy if the challenge of overcoming them is too great for either party: moving away through your – or your partner's – job, being evicted or moving to a rescue centre; changing jobs, redundancy or unemployment; giving up work to have a family; mental health problems such as depression; having a great change in fortune – either by becoming bankrupt or winning or inheriting a vast sum, or marrying someone your friends don't like.

# 4

# ROLES, RELATIONSHIPS AND GOOD SOCIAL PRACTICE

Relationships are varied and ever changing – they can improve or deteriorate, start afresh or disintegrate at any time – and the feelings experienced within a relationship are individual to the person experiencing them: two people who are friends with a third person will not feel exactly the same about this third person, nor will that third person feel the same about the other two. This is what makes friendships special and personal: but it also makes it difficult to have hard and fast rules.

By understanding the role you have to play, and by learning what works and doesn't work with a particular person, you become skilled at dealing with her. But how you deal with another person might be very different. You also need to know how to behave when you are at different places and when and where is the best time to say and do things. Roles, personality and accepted social practices add to the complexity of relationships, which makes it understandable that so many often get it wrong. By becoming more knowledgeable, you can lessen the likelihood of making mistakes and become increasingly skilled at dealing with others.

## Roles in relationships

Some relationships are equal – such as with friends who are equally likely to initiate an outing, or a couple who fairly share responsibilities – but others rely on father/son, mother/son, father/daughter, mother/daughter roles that are unequal. For example, a young woman having a friend in her fifties may look to that woman for motherly advice and have a mother/daughter relationship with her. A friendship where one friend is more dominant – such as through being more experienced or confident – is workable only if both of the people concerned are comfortable with this. Sometimes this shift is temporary such as when one friend is bereaved and the other takes charge until the bereaved person can cope again. But a time when this might not be a comfortable relationship is when one of the friends takes advantage of his superior influence and bullies the other person.

In a marriage, some men prefer to have a wife or partner in a motherly role so that she cooks, cleans, washes and irons for him and takes out the drudgery of everyday living. This works well if his partner is also of the opinion that she wants to behave in a motherly way. If not, there will be conflict and the relationship may fail. Another unequal marriage role pair is when a woman wants a father figure for her partner, preferring to have a 'little girl' role of being looked after, being made to feel secure as she was when she was at home – or as she would have liked it to have been. This works only if her partner enjoys being the powerful father figure who sees she is safe and well cared for.

Examples of other unequal roles in life include teacher/pupil, tutor/tutee, boss/employee, doctor/patient, mother-in-law/daughter-in-law, uncle/nephew, therapist/client, landlord/tenant and waiter/customer. The relationships in these roles work from the basis that the roles are meant to be unequal. Some roles are artificially created for the environment in which the relationship is carried out, such as with the waiter/customer relationship; but with others, such as the uncle/nephew relationship, the role pair holds for wherever they are.

## Roles and expected behaviour

People behave differently according to the situation they are in and the role they are playing. If your behaviour does not satisfy certain expectations difficulties of acceptance may arise, or you may find yourself in trouble in other ways.

*In the host/guest relationship*, the role of the host is to make guests feel welcome and at ease. The host should greet the guest when he arrives, take his coat and offer him a drink. Then he should be introduced to others and left to chat while the host sees to other guests. At the time of departure, the host should see the guest to the door and thank him for coming. If the host does not take care of his guest in this way, he will not feel welcome and will be offended.

The role of the guest is to be polite and grateful for being invited round. Sometimes it is appropriate to take wine and chocolate or flowers for the host, especially if invited to dinner. The guest is expected to talk to others and make himself as agreeable as possible; he should not leave without thanking the host. He should ring the host the following day to say how much he had enjoyed the evening but if he also stayed overnight, he should thank his host by letter. If he doesn't do this, he may be considered rude and ungrateful.

*In the speaker/audience relationship* the role of the speaker is to deliver a carefully prepared speech, talk loud and clear enough to be understood, with any slides, transparencies or computer-generated presentations easily visible to all. Her speech should be as interesting as possible and delivered within the given time frame. If she overruns, people in the audience will look at their watches and fidget; if she finishes too soon and there are no questions, the organiser may not know what to do to fill the gap.

The role of the audience is to listen without fidgeting, talking or coughing, saving questions to the end of the speech unless the speaker has invited members of the audience to interrupt. When asking questions members of the audience should put up their hands and wait to be invited to speak and should be prepared to take their turn. If many want to ask questions, it would be appropriate for a person to ask only one question so that the speaker's time is shared fairly among other members of the audience.

*In the police officer/citizen relationship*, the role of a police officer is to act within the law and to take charge of potentially dangerous situations. In an arrest she should not use more force than the situation warrants and must tell the person she is arresting what rights he has. A citizen should act within the law or be prepared to take the consequences. An offending citizen should allow himself to be arrested without verbal or physical abuse – as this would get him into further trouble.

## Types of relationships
As well as relationships forming role-pairs, each role-pair can be classed into different types of relationship: you relate to others in different ways because of their different standing, and their or your different needs.

*Permanent relationships* include relationships with family and extended family members, your partner and her family, your children and stepchildren and members of a static community, whether neighbours or religious contacts. Role-pairs include: parent/child, grandparent/grandchild, aunt/niece, neighbour/neighbour, priest/lay person. Some friend/friend relationships are also permanent.

*Temporary relationships* include relationships with colleagues and bosses, new friends and partners – you don't yet know if they will become a permanent part of your life. Role-pairs include: colleague/colleague, employer/employee, friend/friend.

*Relationships to satisfy particular needs.* To be well served by your relationships you need to have a mixture of permanent and temporary relationships that include many different role-pairs. For example, if you only have friend/friend relationships without family role-pairs, you might feel vulnerable in times of crises: young orphans know that they must have strong friendships as there may be no one else to fall back on in times of need. As a middle-aged person, you may still feel vulnerable when your parents have died as you are now the oldest in the family whom others look to for support.

The social network mentioned in Chapter 2 only included friendships, but there are obviously far more people with whom you interact and all relationships should be nurtured. So in your ideal social network that is made up of one or more cliques, a looser network and isolated friends, you also should aim to have various needs satisfied to give you maximum social support and reward. These needs include:

- Being nurtured (child/parent).
- Nurturing (parent/child).
- Befriending (including: friend/friend, sibling/sibling, cousin/cousin) for mutual support.
- Crisis management (as befriending and grandchild/grandparent, child/parent, employee/employer, neighbour/neighbour, acquaintance/acquaintance, lay person/priest, patient/doctor) to pull out all the stops to help you through a short-lived crisis. After the crisis is over, the level of support and contact will probably drop to what it was before the crisis.
- Informational help (as crisis management but also role-pairs such as member/librarian, friend's

acquaintance/friend's acquaintance, colleague's child/ father's colleague, caller/helpline worker). In other words anyone who can help at all, and you don't need to know them personally.
- Romance and love (partner/partner).

### Good social practice

Whatever role you are in at the time, there are always certain social expectations that are not role-specific. Your manner can be misinterpreted as rude if you don't behave according to the expectations of the culture you are in and exhibit the appropriate social skills.

On greeting others be prepared to make eye contact, give a big welcoming smile and offer your hand or be prepared to offer it quickly when the other person offers his. A firm handshake is required rather than pumping or limp ones. However, these are appropriate with some people from other cultures: Australians tend to give hearty pumping handshakes and Asians rather limp handshakes.

First impressions count for much as people decide within the first couple of minutes whether they like you, so it would be a mistake to appear critical or judgmental, or show surprise, disgust or shock at the other person's appearance should there be something unexpected such as an acute case of acne or a badly scarred face. If the person has a very obvious problem it is best not to keep trying to avoid looking or skirting round the subject. For example, if someone's face has been badly burned and looks as though the person has undergone numerous skin grafts, you could gently say something like, 'What happened to you?' However, this should not be the first thing you utter. Save it until you have been chatting for a while. Don't try to escape from a person just because you feel embarrassed about a defect. Accept it as they must and see beyond to the person inside.

During the course of your interaction you should remember to:

- Judge the other person's mood. Whether it is playful or serious, respond in kind. Try to be flexible.
- Value the other person and treat her with respect. If you do this she will respect you back and will be more open to what you have to say.
- Show genuine interest without being manipulative. For example, you should not talk to someone at a party for the sole purpose of hoping he will benefit your career or boost company profits.

In taking interest it is good to try to remember the other person's name and follow the conversation: the next time you meet, you can show how genuinely interested you were by, for example, asking after important events that were looming in her life such as the funeral of an aunt, the wedding of a son or the birth of her first grandchild.

You also need to be alert and sensitive to the situation. For example, if you have taken up an acquaintance's offer of calling on him for the first time, much depends on his reaction when he finds you on his doorstep. If he doesn't look pleased to see you, you will feel uncomfortable and will know that he probably didn't really mean you to call. Or it may be that you have called at a bad time and he cannot hide the fact although he denies it's inconvenient. Either of these scenarios is likely to make you want to cut short your visit and never call again.

However, if he were to look genuinely pleased to see you and wholeheartedly welcome you while saying how delighted he is that you came, you are likely to feel at ease and be happy to stay for some time, not overly worrying about outstaying your welcome. Even if it is inconvenient, he could still look delighted to see you, say he can only spare a few minutes and why, and then offer to make an arrangement to see you again when he can give you undivided attention.

Good manners are another social essential: think of them as oiling the wheels of social interactions.

- Always thank hosts for a lovely time and compliment them on the food. Try to think of something genuine to say even if it is hard, as it shows when compliments are insincere.
- Refrain from pointing (this is acceptable in Chinese society but is rude in Western society), picking your nose (this is perfectly acceptable in public in Thailand, but not in Western society), belching (which is expected in Arab societies), farting, picking the dirt from under your nails, picking spots, eating with your mouth open and talking with your mouth full of food.
- Don't discuss toilet habits, vomiting, diarrhoea and medical procedures while at the table.
- Don't over-disclose for the level of acquaintanceship you have with the other person. An example is talking about your partner's infidelities or his lack of mobile sperm for procreation when you've only just met her.
- Don't over-disclose in an inappropriate environment such as in church during a service or at a formal business event.
- However much alcohol there might be on offer at a social occasion, if you want to make a good impression you should not imbibe so much that you become bawdy, morose, violent or sick.
- Be sensitive to the environment you are in: avoid talking about depressing subjects when at a party or any celebratory event as this will spoil the atmosphere; at a funeral you should be sombre; at college or a meeting you should be attentive.
- Be sensitive to the people around you and don't make crass jokes for the hell of it. An example might be going up to someone who looks shocked and saying

in a loud voice, 'What's up? Seen a ghost?' Then, too late, you find out that someone close to her has just died. Use your levity with people you know well and where you're not likely to blunder.

# 5

# CONVERSATION

Successful conversations are two-way events where both parties feel valued and rewarded. Without conversation, you would find it hard to develop or maintain any relationship or live your life effectively: you need people to communicate with you whether, for example, it's to ask for help with your tax assessment or to explain your side of an argument, and it's the easiest way to let others get to know you and you them.

### Uses of conversation

How you use conversation tells others a great deal about you and contributes to your personal identity.

*Using conversation to develop intimacy* is useful in building bonds between you and another person. You can develop intimacy by showing that you can empathise, sympathise, confide personal information, find common ground (such as in life experiences or situations), level out differences, avoid abuse of positions such as employer over employee, and to reach a greater understanding of the other person.

*Using conversation to develop control/show superiority* is useful when, for example, you feel it is necessary for someone to 'know his place' and show it by the way you talk to him. This might be as a parent, boss or teacher.

*Using conversation to show inferiority* is useful when you are in a subordinate position at work. For example, you might want to show your eagerness to cooperate by readily accepting orders, and by asking permission to do something. However, you might go too far either in the workplace or socially, by being too ready to apologise and take the blame, making you vulnerable to bullying.

*Using conversation to give information* is vital, for example, when you are an employer having a meeting with your staff, an employee explaining why something was finished late, a doctor explaining how to take medicine, a mother explaining the dangers of fire to her children, and a teacher needing to educate and inform.

*Using conversation to show independence* does the opposite of developing intimacy: it emphasises the differences between you rather than recognising commonalities. You can show independence by, for example, making it clear you are capable of doing something by yourself or by admitting that something has happened but you don't want to discuss it. You can also show defiance, such as by stating that you are going to do something with or without the other person's permission, although this is likely to create conflict.

## Conversation cues

To be an effective conversationalist, you need constantly to read your audience's body language. This will tell you if the other person is interested in what you have to say and whether she is enjoying your company. You must also be careful about your own body language; it needs to be positive and relaxed.

To have positive conversation body language showing you are interested in the other person, you need to look confident and smile when appropriate, particularly on meeting him; lean towards him and have your body completely facing him; make plenty of eye contact; nod to show agreement; make small comments such as, 'Really?' or 'I've not heard that one before' to show that you are paying attention, and repeat back anything you are unsure of to check your understanding and to show him you are listening: 'You mean . . .?'

Conversation cues to look for, showing you when people aren't interested in what you have to say, include yawning, looking over their shoulder or around the room for someone more interesting to talk to or for a means of escape, turning their body to one side so that they do not face you squarely, trying to change the subject and regularly checking their watch. If you have to look at your watch because you have an appointment or you have to look over someone's shoulder because you'd arranged to meet someone else, then explain this to the person you are talking to so that he does not feel uncomfortable about your body language.

When someone is trying to leave a conversation, watch out for body language cues that include turning her body away from you, moving backwards and making signs such as picking up keys, handbag or papers and putting on her coat. (Also see below.)

### Conversations with strangers

Everyone needs to speak to people they have never met before at some time. The conversation might only last a few seconds, such as with someone serving you in a shop, but the rewards are still there. Practise your conversational skills and take advantage of every opportunity of meeting people – just for fun. You will then find it easier to talk to others when it really does matter.

*Start a conversation* by smiling, saying hello and remembering some of the suggestions given below – but you must ensure your voice is loud enough to be heard without shouting: it is very embarrassing if you have to repeat a greeting.

Your chosen subjects should involve both of you: where you are or things that you have in common such as families and hobbies. You will have to ask questions to find out about them. Volunteer information at the same level you have asked the other person – or wait to see if that person asks you a similar question back. If she never does, you will have to keep the conversation balanced by giving it freely yourself.

Stick to general comments anyone can listen to. Don't make it a private or secret conversation – unless you have both found out you hate, for example, the party you are at and are making plans to leave together to find somewhere more interesting to go. Don't go in for heavy, emotional conversations at a first meeting or asking intimate questions. For example, it implies you might want to chat someone up if your first question is, 'Are you married?' Also avoid asking questions of the other person you wouldn't be prepared to answer yourself; for example, how much he earns. In Western cultures this is usually a taboo subject, even among friends, so is a totally inappropriate question to ask strangers. But it is not so in Japan as the Japanese like to know what a person is earning early on in the relationship to know how deferential to be: the person who earns less must bow lower when greeting.

Try not to ask questions in a clumsy way. For example, if you are at a work's party and can't understand why there's a complete stranger there, don't ask, 'Why are *you* here?' but say, 'What's your connection with the company?'

*Talk about the immediacy of the situation*
- Am I late?
- Have you been here before?
- How do you know the host? How long have you known him?
- Unusual weather, don't you think?
- You don't sound as though you're from this area.

*Talk about family and pets*
- Do you have brothers and sisters?
- What family do you have?
- Do you have children?
- Do you have any pets?
- I am a dog lover. Do you like dogs?

*Talk about jobs*
- How do you spend your time?/Do you work?
- Did it take you a long time to get qualified?
- Where do you work? How long does it take you to get to work?

*Talk about hobbies and leisure time*
- What do you do with your spare time?/Do you have any hobbies?
- Have you always lived here?
- Do you play any sport?
- Are you interested in football?/Have you been following the football on television?

*Talk about education*
- Where did you go to school?
- When did you leave school?
- Did you go on to further education?
- Have you had any special training?

*Keep the conversation going:* sometimes the first few questions are easy to ask and give answers to but then the conversation dries up so prepare a bank of topics to talk about – such as personal information asked about in Chapter 1 and about local interests, which can be remembered from your local newspaper. Don't mumble – if the person has to strain to hear you she might give up and try to escape to find someone easier to talk to. Give information about yourself without always having to be asked and allow some pauses in the conversation for the other person to have a say. Look for questions to ask when the other person gives information about himself to allow delving – then the conversation isn't just a series of very superficial unrelated questions and, by doing this, you are more likely to find things in common. Make a comment on something the other person says: you could offer sympathy or congratulations or say you'd have done the same or tell a similar story to show you've experienced the same thing.

*End the conversation* without offending the other person. Explain why you must go: 'I've got a train to catch' or, 'I've arranged to meet someone' or, 'I've got an appointment.' Say, 'I'm pleased to have met you' and, 'Perhaps we'll see each other again some time.' If you enjoyed talking to her, say so. If she told you about a forthcoming event say, 'Good luck with . . . your exam/your daughter's wedding/your job interview.' If she told you she was feeling unwell, say, 'I hope you feel better soon.' Shake hands – if appropriate: usually you only need to do this if you've been formally introduced.

If you are finding it hard to free yourself from the conversation add body language to your verbal comment about needing to leave: pick up your things, stand up if sitting, step back while turning your body away and give a final goodbye and smile and then turn fully away and leave. If you feel you are leaving very hastily and wish to temper your abrupt departure, lightly touch the other person's arm as you apologise about leaving in such a rush.

### Conversations with people you have met before

Conversations with people you have met before are easier than with strangers because you already have some idea about the other person and what interests him.

It is common when you first meet someone after a break to ask after his health and then other things you have talked about before such as his family, job and hobbies, and to admire any changes such as a haircut, a smart suit and to comment on how well he looks. If you have warning about meeting him, you can remind yourself in advance about the last conversation you had and anything you should ask about. Recall family members' names, where he lives and works and the names of other people he has mentioned and any troubles he had: it makes it easier to pick up where you left off.

Have some ideas on what you would like to say about yourself: if you do not know the other person well, think of mainly positive things to say to keep the conversation light. Although you mustn't burden an unsuspecting person with all your worries, be prepared to give away some things; saying everything is 'fine' does not allow the conversation to flow and there may be awkward silences while one of you works out the next question. Also give more than one word answers.

As a safety measure think up general topics that you would be able to discuss comfortably, without causing an argument, between either of you. If you and the other person have other friends in common remind yourself of any confidences you must keep: either information about another person or anything you have heard about the person you are going to meet. If the person you meet tells you something you already know but have to keep quiet about knowing, pretend he is telling you the news for the first time.

### Conversation rules

Even when talking to others there are rules and expectations. For example, it is impolite to interrupt someone speaking unless it is for an emergency. Sometimes you are expected to wait your turn or give others a chance to voice their opinions. You also need to show sensitivity and awareness of the situation you are in. For example, if someone has died, you are expected to speak more softly to show respect and to sound sympathetic to mourners, whereas at a disco you are at liberty to shout as loud as you want to make your voice heard above the music.

*Group conversation.* Be careful that you don't cut people out from your conversation because you talk about things that automatically exclude them. If you know that you have things in common with all group members bar one, it would be polite to avoid those topics or to ask if the other person has interests in them. Saying, 'And what sort of wine will you be buying from Bordeaux this year?' can have a double edge to it if the person left out knows nothing about wine *and* is on a relatively low income.

When a third person arrives while you are mid-conversation with someone else, you must acknowledge his arrival by smiling or saying hello and, if necessary, introduce him to your companion. Either update him on the conversation underway so that he can join in or abandon the first conversation for the time being and start a new one with which he can join in. However, if you do abandon the first conversation, you must find the opportunity to finish it later. This attempt to include the new arrival may not work if your companion is not receptive to being interrupted in this way and if the new arrival cannot wait for the first conversation to come to a natural close: he might leave.

*Conversation no-nos.* If you want to be successful in your conversation and win the other person's approval, avoid the following pitfalls:

- Don't interrupt other people's conversations. If you've heard it all before, keep quiet. Don't say, 'I've heard it before and I can't bear to listen to it again' or, 'I know that already.'

- Don't try to guess the ending of another person's sentence – unless that person often struggles for words and you know he'd appreciate help. Let him finish in his own way and in his own time.

- Don't try to change the subject because you're embarrassed about what is being said or you're bored with that line of conversation or because you think you've got something far more interesting to say. These all tell the other person that she is uninteresting because you can't wait to change the subject. Let the conversation come to a natural finish before changing the subject.

- Understand the other person's manner. Some people have longer pauses between sentences than others, which can be cultural, or due to the way they were brought up. Don't try to fill in the gaps or take control of the conversation. Accept the slower pace and try to adapt to it even if you feel there is a pressure of time.

- Don't try to force the pace of the conversation. For example, many people like to have preamble as a starter before the main course of the conversation, which includes asking people how they are and how their journey was. To jump straight in to business, whether at work or leisure, before others are satisfied that the niceties have been completed will look clumsy and busy-bodying. If others don't appear to notice that time is pressured, you should try to follow suit.

- Don't try to dominate the conversation. Let others have a turn and don't be too quick to take up the reins again. Show that everyone present is valued and can have his say. Be prepared to be quiet at times. Always being the centre of attention and dictating what others should talk about breaks down rapport and shows you are insensitive.

# 6

# CONVERSATION AND PERSONALITY

There are several types of personality evident in conversation that can be considered boring and not allowing the other person to become involved. These are described below. The first four descriptions apply to confident people – note that because someone is confident, it does not make her socially competent as some shy people might think. The last description applies to unconfident people.

*'Know-all'* I came across a know-all at a Bed and Breakfast in an old, converted mill. When the last family came in to eat, the father said good morning to everyone in the room before taking his seat. Immediately he got up again to look at the old mill wheel that was in its original place, the breakfast room having been built around it. He called to his children to come and look and began to describe the workings of the mill at normal voice volume so that everyone could easily hear. When the owner came to take his breakfast order he asked her if her dog was called Dusty after Dusty Miller – from an old British children's programme – and she said it was.

He had shown everyone in the room he was very confident, could take the lead, was not intimidated by his surroundings and enjoyed showing off his knowledge to all: none of his conversations was *sotto voce*; he had expected everyone to hear and take note.

*'I've got to be right'* Joanne, working in the legal profession, has many opinions on a range of subjects and expects her partner and children to hold them too, confident about them being the right opinion. Once her views are formed, she rarely changes them. If another person's opinion accords perfectly with her own, she tells him how right he is and bestows warm and encouraging looks, but if it differs she points out flaws or bluntly refuses to agree with him, considering him stupid for not seeing it her way. If she is proved wrong, she becomes hostile and can't openly admit to, or apologise for, her mistake.

Joanne is often tempted to give advice even when it is not in her area of expertise or knowledge just so that she can show the other person she has the answers and is always right.

*'I'm better than anyone'* Ralph, a banker, assumes an air of boredom in conversation as though he can't be bothered to engage fully, believing the others around him are not very clever or worthy of his attention. He feels it is commendable to keep himself from wasting time with people who have nothing to offer, but his attitude keeps most people away, blocking them from achieving any intimacy with him. He is lonely and largely disliked, only on the fringes of whatever is happening around him. Others rarely seek his help, as he is unfriendly and looks down on them considering their intellect, social status and views on life inferior to his.

Ralph has many prejudices and only shows approval if others conform to his views and way of life – his religion and culture, the way he brings up his children, the values he holds regarding health and education, the type of food he eats, etc. It boosts his ego when he feels he's got the better of someone else and never worries about the other person's loss of face or how he makes her feel about herself.

*'I want to know all about you'* Martha, when introduced to people, relentlessly questions them about details of their personal life without volunteering a single piece of information about herself or by talking about things in general. Asking whether they are single, where they live, who their family are and fishing about how much they earn are inappropriate questions for complete strangers, but Martha likes to know these things to compare how she is doing against the people she meets, feeling comforted if someone is worse off in some way and feeling resentful if they are better off. She does not notice other people's increasing discomfort under her grilling. The only thing on her mind is to satisfy her curiosity: there is no realisation that conversation is a two-way thing, or that both sides need to gain something from the conversation to make it rewarding and balanced.

*'I'd prefer not to be noticed'* At a pre-interview evening I attended with my husband to meet other candidates and staff, another woman accompanying her husband in relation to the same job application caught my attention. She was obviously overwhelmed by the entire situation: she couldn't lift her eyes from the floor and her body language was extremely uncomfortable, sitting with shoulders hunched, legs crossed and arms tightly close to her body while her husband stood beside her, chatting to potential colleagues. Throughout the evening she remained unsmilingly seated, keeping her gaze averted, making no attempt to join in any conversation. Neither did her husband try to include her. When someone did address her, she mumbled a brief reply with her gaze only briefly lifting from the floor.

Since the job involved living in company accommodation with everyone else who worked in the institution, spouses and partners were considered to be part of the package; they had to be able to fit in. Although it was important for this woman to pretend she was at ease and to appear confident, she couldn't. It was no surprise to me that her husband was not offered to fill one of the three vacancies.

### Conversations in practice

The following scripts illustrate how a conversation might be affected by someone's personality. Throughout, Alys stays the same person but Dave becomes whichever personality he is portraying at the time. The ways the conversations develop, or don't develop, depend on the particular personality Dave has: Alys reacts differently to each because of how he talks to her and it becomes clear how certain behaviour blocks a friendly repartee forming; something which is essential for meeting new people and dating.

*It is a pleasantly warm day and Alys is sitting on one end of a park bench looking at the duck pond with her toddler son Jamie strapped into his pushchair beside her when Dave comes to sit at the other end of the bench.*

### 'Know-all'

Dave:    (Sits down at the end of the bench. Looks around him and puffs himself up ready for a conversation with the woman at the other end because he is bored and can spare the time to be diverted.) It's very pleasant here. Sitting by water, particularly running water, is supposed to be very relaxing. Good for the psyche.

Alys:    (Smiles and makes eye contact.) It is.

Dave:    This time last year there were heavy storms that flooded the cottages at the end of the lane. Took weeks to dry them out. Ridiculous place to have built them of course, so close to the river, and in a dip. It's obvious that they'd flood with a heavy downpour. Anyone can see it's the wrong place to build.

Alys:    They hadn't flooded before and as they've stood there for over a hundred years, it is reasonable to suppose that they could last a bit longer.

Dave:    (He snorts.) Maybe they were safe then. But with the weather changing from global warming anyone who buys one of them would be making a terrible investment.

Alys:    Not everyone buys for investment. Sometimes all they want is a pleasant home.

Dave:    Having a poky little cottage to live in is not what I'd call pleasant. Maybe OK if you're on your own but not with a family. They'll be hard to sell now. Wouldn't be surprised if the owners want to get shot of them.

Alys:    (Bristling voice.) I live in one of them and I don't want to sell. And they're plenty big enough for a family.

Dave:    (Pointedly looking at the toddler.) You won't say that when the next child comes along.

Alys:    It's just the two of us now. There won't be any more children.

Dave:    If people aren't prepared to take on responsibility, they shouldn't have children. It's not fair on the child to be left with only one parent. Children need both parents for a balanced family and to act as good role models. And then there's the drain on the Department for Work and Pensions. I hope the Child Support Agency is on to him.

(Jamie starts to struggle to be let out of the pushchair and points excitedly to the family of ducks that is approaching. Alys lets him out and fishes in the bag of the pushchair for some bread.)

Dave:    You're not supposed to feed bread to the ducks. It makes them ill.

Alys:    (Pauses. Then hands her child the bread.) There isn't a sign up. And we come here regularly to feed them. No one's ever said anything before.

Dave:    Well, it's true. They're designed to eat grass and invertebrates, not bread: Mallards are surface feeders. They're important in some parts of the world because they eat mosquito larvae that float on water. If you feed ducks bread they become tame and so lose their natural ability to protect themselves and shy away from danger. It also means that there's an over-abundance of food so other ducks come and then they get overcrowded. Then their waste builds up and bacteria from it kills the fish. They rot and create more bacteria that harm humans. Plus the animals that feed on the fish starve. And it interferes with the ducks' migration. They don't migrate if they're fed too well.

Alys:    (Gets up with Jamie and wanders close to the water to feed the ducks without a backward glance.)

*Alys gives the minimum answer when she dislikes what Dave says. And at the end she ignores him altogether. She doesn't need an acquaintance as opinionated as him. Also, his company is boring and unrewarding. He was only interested in showing off his knowledge, preferring to talk at Alys rather than to her.*

**'I've got to be right'**

Dave:    (Sits down at the end of the bench.) Enjoying a long lunch break?

Alys:    (Smiles and makes eye contact.) Sort of.

Dave:    You don't work I expect, with having the little one to look after?

Alys:    (Defensively.) No.

Dave:    It's good for one of the parents to stay at home
         to bring up the child. It's the best start in life for
         them.

Alys:    I know that, but not everyone can afford to.

Dave:    No. But when they can. And that's what you've
         chosen to do isn't it? It's worth the sacrifice of
         having two incomes.

Alys:    I haven't even got one income actually. And
         what do you know about it? Have you got
         children?

Dave:    Not yet. Got that pleasure to come. Your first is
         he?

Alys:    Yes.

Dave:    If you have the next one soon, they'll be close
         enough in age to play nicely together.

Alys:    (Silent for a while.) There won't be a next one.

Dave:    You'll change your mind in time. Most people
         do.

Alys:    (Brittle voice.) Sometimes it's not a matter of
         choice.

Dave:    Husband doesn't want another?

Alys:    I don't have a husband.

Dave:    I thought you must be a single parent. Left you
         did he?
         (Jamie starts to struggle to be let out of the
         pushchair and points excitedly to the family of
         ducks that is approaching. Alys lets him out and
         fishes in the bag of the pushchair for some
         bread.)

Dave:    Feeding bread to the ducks makes them ill.

Alys:    (Pauses. Then hands her child the bread.) There
         isn't a sign up. And we come here regularly to
         feed them. No one's ever said anything before.

Dave:    Well, it's truc. It's not what they're supposed to
         eat. I've seen signs up all over Europe asking

people not to feed them – but for some reason they don't do it here. You ask any expert. He'll tell you.

Alys:       (Ignores him and continues to let her child feed the ducks that are coming eagerly towards them.)

*Alys ignores Dave when he asks if her husband left her. Dave uses the conversation not to get to know Alys but as a game to see if he can correctly sum her up. He doesn't notice her annoyed responses or the fact that he is being very insensitive. He assumes he was correct about Alys' husband leaving her so moves on to talk about the ducks. Note how he automatically labels the expert as male. At the end of the conversation Dave will be pleased with himself for being so astute about this complete stranger.*

### 'I'm better than anyone'

Dave:       (Sits down at the end of the bench.)

Alys:       (Looks over and smiles at him.) It's so pleasant here isn't it?

Dave:       (Distractedly.) Mm. It's a rare thing for me to fritter my time away like this. I'm usually too busy to indulge. I run my own business.

Alys:       Really?

Dave:       Oh yes. It's a building company. I'm a surveyor. I advise on where to build and not to build and check out buildings for mortgage companies. And assess damage like with those cottages that were flooded last year, although my company wasn't involved that time. Rather unfortunate place to have them although it must have seemed like a good idea at the time. (He laughs.)

Alys:       (Suppressed anger.) I live in one of them.

Dave:       Poor you. Not worth much now I'd think. People know to ask now whether a house has been flooded and it being so near the river . . . Housewife are you?

Alys:        (Bristling.) Not exactly. But I don't work.

Dave:        Not someone else who's draining the country's resources through the Department for Work and Pensions? You should try working – you'll get more money. Then you won't have time to get bored.

Alys:        (Irritation and anger in her voice.) I'll return to work when Jamie has a place at nursery. And I'm not bored.

Dave:        Well, if you were terribly busy, you wouldn't have time to come here.

Alys:        Children need to be taken out for fresh air, exercise and stimulation.

             (Jamie starts to struggle to be let out of the pushchair and points excitedly to the family of ducks that is approaching. Alys lets him out and fishes in the bag of the pushchair for some bread.)

Dave:        I don't feed the ducks as it makes them ill. Not many people know it in the UK but it is widely known in Europe. You should tell all your friends not to let their kids feed them bread. It's the fault of today's education system. People are leaving school without having learnt anything. Can barely read or write some of them. Unemployed and unemployable.

Alys:        (Pauses. Then hands her child the bread. She moves away, one hand on the pushchair and the other holding Jamie's hand and walks to the furthest point of the pond, the ducks following noisily.)

*Alys voted with her feet here and left Dave's unrewarding and upsetting company. He's assuming too much about her (that she's living off benefits, that she's bored, that she regrets living in her cottage, that she's not well educated and that all her friends must be women with children – probably single women with children). She is under no obligation to put him right as that would reveal personal information that he has no right to have or expect to have.*

### 'I want to know all about you'

Dave: Hello. Do you mind if I sit here?

Alys: (Smiles and makes eye contact.) No.

Dave: Do you come here often?

Alys: A fair bit.

Dave: I've never seen you here before – but then I'm too busy to come much. You a housewife?

Alys: Sort of.

Dave: (Laughs.) What does that mean?

Alys: I'm a homemaker but there's no husband so I can't be a housewife.

Dave: I see. You're a single mum.

Alys: Yes.

Dave: How old's the child?

Alys: Two.

Dave: When did he leave?

Alys: Pardon?

Dave: Your boyfriend? When did he leave you?

Alys: He wasn't my boyfriend, he –

Dave: I see. Did you plan to have a baby on your own then?

Alys: (Irritated voice.) I'm sorry, but how come you're so interested?

Dave: (Affronted.) Just making conversation ... I expect it's hard living off a low income. Where do you live?

Alys: None of your business!

(Jamie starts to struggle to be let out of the pushchair and points excitedly to the family of ducks that is approaching. Alys lets him out and fishes in the bag of the pushchair for some bread.)

Dave:  Did you know that you're not supposed to feed bread to the ducks? It's well known in Europe that you shouldn't. Have you been abroad? Or is the language a barrier for you? Or perhaps you can't afford it . . .

Alys:  (Gets up and pushes the buggy to another part of the pond and then helps Jamie feed the ducks.)

*Alys leaves Dave's company as he's more than overstepped polite boundaries. His questions were very intrusive and only someone who knows Alys intimately should ask things about when she planned to have her baby. He also assumes far too much about her. Note that Dave did not volunteer any information about himself to make the conversation less of an inquisition.*


**'I'd prefer not to be noticed'**

Dave:  (Sits down on the other end of the bench.)

Alys:  (Smiles at him.) It's pleasant here, isn't it?

Dave:  (Quickly looks at her and away again.) Sorry?

Alys:  I was just saying, it's very pleasant here.

Dave:  Oh. Mm. (He studies his hands and then looks at the pond.)

Alys:  I try to come whenever I can.

Dave:  Oh.

Alys:  Do you come here much?

Dave:  No.

Alys:  I find it's so much nicer than sitting at home. And it gives Jamie a change of scene.

Dave:  (Silence.)

Alys:  (Gives up and talks to Jamie and gets him out of the pushchair to feed the ducks.)

*Alys gave Dave several opportunities to engage in conversation. Very shy behaviour (or socially inhibited behaviour) does not allow for meeting new people.*

When you start a conversation with a complete stranger, it does not mean the other person will interpret it as a chat-up. If you get on well with a stranger and the person wants to make the boundaries clear, he or she soon introduces the subject of a partner and children, if present. And you can too, if you have them so that each of you can relax.

In the conversation below, note how a skilled conversationalist can have a rewarding and well-balanced conversation and how much easier it is to find out about others and get them to talk about themselves when they treat the other with respect and in a non-judgmental way.

### 'Skilled conversationalist'

| | |
|---|---|
| Dave: | Do you mind if I sit here? |
| Alys: | (Smiles and makes eye contact.) No. |
| Dave: | Enjoying a long lunch break? |
| Alys: | (Smiles and makes eye contact.) Sort of. |
| Dave: | Me too . . . This time last year there were thunderstorms that flooded the cottages at the end of the lane. Took weeks to dry them out. |
| Alys: | I know. Mine was one of them. How do you know it took weeks? |
| Dave: | I read it in the paper. I'm sorry you got flooded. |
| Alys: | Me too. I was in quite a mess for ages. It took so long for the insurance money to come through and we couldn't live there for weeks and weeks. |
| Dave: | I'm a surveyor so I'm interested in sizing up buildings and assessing damage. |
| Alys: | We had one of those when we took out our mortgage – as well as after the flood, of course. |
| Dave: | I bet you find it hard now that you've got a child. Did you have to give up work? |
| Alys: | (Nods.) I was a teacher. I hope to go back when Jamie's old enough to go to nursery. And it's the |

best career I could have had when I've got a child to bring up.

Dave:      So Dad's supporting you both?

Alys:      I wish. He died last year.

Dave:      I'm so sorry.

Alys:      (She blinks back tears.) Thanks.

Dave:      I found it really hard when my Mum died. I was only seventeen. It took me years to get over it. I'm not sure you ever do entirely – but it gets easier.

Alys:      (Nods and fishes for a tissue to wipe her eyes and blow her nose.)

Dave:      Hey, I'm sorry I've upset you.

Alys:      No. It's OK. It's your sympathy that did it. It's nice to have someone to talk to.

Dave:      (He offers his hand.) I'm Dave.

Alys:      (She shakes his hand and smiles at him.) Alys. (Jamie starts to struggle to be let out of the pushchair and points excitedly to the family of ducks that is approaching. Alys lets him out and fishes in the bag of the pushchair for some bread.)

Dave:      I might be wrong but I thought feeding bread to the ducks could make them ill.

Alys:      Oh. No one's said anything before. (Her hand hovers uncertainly over the bread.) What do they eat then?

Dave:      Stuff on the surface of the water – and grass. (Jamie puts his hand out to take the bread and makes impatient noises.)

Dave:      I think you'd better let him feed them. It would be a shame to disappoint him.

Alys:      (Laughs.) OK. Would you like some bread?

Dave:      (Laughs too.) Why not? Brings back childhood memories. I'm told we never really grow up.

*Dave tries to find common ground to balance the relationship. He admits to having a long lunch break when Alys partially admits to it. Instead of trying to point out differences as the unskilled but confident conversationalists did, he tries to find areas of commonality. Because Dave's been gentle with Alys and not opinionated or judgmental, she is more ready to listen to his tentative comment about the bread being bad for the ducks as shown by her hand hovering uncertainly over it. Only when Dave gives her 'permission' to continue is she happy about feeding it to the ducks.*

Good conversation is like dancing with someone where each person has a chance to take the lead and each person has a chance to be led.

# 7

# LISTENING AND CARING SKILLS

When listening and caring skills are used by professionals it is known as counselling; when used by lay-people they can enhance relationships socially, at home and at work, and can earn you respect. However, there are certain qualities you need to portray and certain skills you need to foster to make you a good listener.

### Listening qualities that help achieve intimacy

*Be respectful* by being courteous and showing interest. Ask, 'Are you warm enough?' and, 'Can I get you something to drink?' Give your undivided attention, facing the other person squarely and leaning forward from the waist, making frequent eye contact, and nodding at appropriate moments to show that you are following what she says. Don't yawn, look bored, display impatience by checking your watch or fiddle with things or your clothes.

*Be empathetic* by showing you understand that the other person is having a hard time – try to put yourself in his shoes and think how you might feel under the same circumstances. Say, 'That must be very hard for you', or 'I expect anyone would find that hard to deal with', but don't suggest you know exactly how he is feeling as you are not him. You might also be able to say that something similar has happened to you, but don't give details as you are the one listening to what he has to say.

*Be sympathetic* by saying things like, 'Oh, that must have been dreadful. Tell me about it,' in a warm, caring and considerate way. Look concerned for the other person and perhaps touch her arm or give her a hug. Don't, for example, try to dismiss grief by cracking jokes: 'That's one less to cook for now', 'I always said your cooking was lethal' or, 'Couldn't stand being with you any longer, eh?' or by being flippant: 'Oh, he's kicked the bucket then?', 'I'm surprised he lasted this long' or, 'Oh, I thought he'd died years ago' or by making sweeping statements: 'Time heals', 'You could always have another baby' or, 'It'll sort itself out.' Comments like these are dismissive of her feelings.

Although saying that 'Time heals' may be true, it is not necessarily welcome when a newly bereaved person is in the throes of emotional torment. Equally unhelpful statements about more general problems include: 'Worrying about it won't help' or, 'Pull yourself together' or, 'You'll get over it.' Instead say, 'I'm really sorry this has happened. It must be awful for you' or, 'I feel very worried about you. You've had some dreadful news and I want to be able to take the pain away but I can't. Please let me know if there's anything I can do.' Make sure your voice sounds genuine. Concentrating on someone else's needs which, at that time are greater than your own, may help you overcome any shyness about showing your feelings and the softer side of your nature.

Not showing the right amount of sympathy at the right time such as immediately after the thing has happened, or the first time you see him after the event has occurred, can foster hostility. Ill-considered words can store up great resentment for the future. For example, if one of your employees comes to you to report an accident that was the company's fault, you should be prepared to listen, make a record of it and check whether she needs medical assistance. But if, instead of offering sympathy, you say, after something heavy has fallen on her head, 'I wouldn't have thought there were too many brain cells to damage', you can expect her to feel hurt and antagonistic towards you.

*Be non-judgmental* by not being biased or allowing strong religious or political views to colour your approach to listening. Avoid criticising the other person as it will make him feel worse, especially if he is already distressed, has had a blow to his confidence or has received unfavourable judgmental comments from others. For example, saying, 'What do you expect after what you did?' will not make him warm to you and is likely to result in his avoiding divulging anything else to you.

*Be patient* and let the other person tell you her troubles in her own time, without interrupting or finishing her sentences for her. If you don't have the time to listen at that moment, explain why not and make a slot available so that you can give her your full attention.

*Be tactful* (see Chapter 11) and show sensitivity to the other person's plight so that you don't intensify his distress, making him feel worse.

*Be genuine* by truly wanting to help the other person and being interested in what she has to say. Don't play at being superior; just be her equal and act like a warm and caring friend.

*Look at the problem objectively* by considering it without bias and without allowing your emotions to sway your thinking – when people are upset they can lose their sense of proportion, being so embroiled in their personal mess they cannot isolate individual difficulties. Help the person see his dilemma from a different perspective.

*Relate* to the other person's point of view to build rapport and show you do understand her difficulties and have her interests at heart, without belittling her: don't say,

'Aren't you exaggerating here?' or, 'That's happened to me and it's no big deal' or, 'Loads of people have that problem.' Acknowledge the truth of what she says. Allow her to be the expert in her life and try to understand why she has come to say the things she has rather than dismiss her feelings: being brusque will make her think that you don't want to waste more time on her.

*Summarise what's been said* to let the other person know you have been listening carefully, confirming whether you have understood. It also helps to clarify what was said in your own mind and helps him focus on his muddled thoughts and concentrate on the salient issues.

*Keep confidentiality* by not telling anyone else what you and the other person discussed and by not referring to your conversation when other people are around by, for example, asking if she feels better now, which would result in someone asking what was wrong. You could simply say, 'Hello. How are you?' without giving anyone else reason to think that there is anything behind the question other than a polite enquiry after her health.

*Know the difference between you and the other person.* If you see a solution that would be perfect for you it does not mean it is the answer for him: ask him what he thinks of it or whether he has already tried or considered it. Remember that whatever similarities are apparent to you as an external observer, internally he can be very different from you: your priorities, life values, opinions, etc., are yours and no one else's and just because you hold certain views and have certain priorities it does not necessarily make them right for everyone.

*Know when you're out of your depth.* If a problem the other person has overwhelms you and you have no idea how to help, admit it straight away and make it clear that you are not rejecting her: just that you're not the best person to help with this particular problem.

If the problems are specific to another person, such as

an employer, there may be appropriate channels in the workplace to pursue: she could speak to her employer direct or go through personnel. For serious emotional problems there may be an appropriate help line to seek advice from, or she could ask her doctor for a referral to a counsellor or therapist – you could offer to accompany her to necessary appointments or to ring up help lines on her behalf. Serious difficulties include feelings of worthlessness and depression, which can lead to suicide; an unexpected or unsought pregnancy; eating disorders; anxiety disorders and panic attacks; rape, sexual or other kinds of abuse; problems with sexuality and the fear of 'coming out', and prolonged grief following bereavement where she can't move on or pick up her life again.

Sometimes you might feel out of your depth because you are hearing disturbing information. If that happens, tell her that you can't help with the problem: she must ask to be referred to a professional counsellor. You may have to talk over the things you have heard with someone else, without divulging names or identifying details, to offload the stress of the disturbing information you were given.

## Listening skills that help achieve intimacy

*Ask open questions* so that the other person cannot give a yes/no answer: 'How are you?', 'When did it happen?', 'How do you feel about that?', 'What makes you think that?', 'Why do you feel so bad?' and 'Where were you when this happened?' (Closed questions and comments include: 'Things OK with you?', 'I expect you're relieved that's all over now', 'Did you enjoy that?', 'Did you have a good day at work?' and 'Are things better now?')

*Check your understanding* by repeating back the information you have been given such as by saying, 'You mean that was the third time that something like this has happened?'

*Listen for openers.* Maureen confided in another parent

that her daughter felt lonely in her group since his daughter had been moved up a class. He replied that she wasn't the only one who was lonely. Had she been single and wanted to find out more, she'd have said, 'You're lonely?'

Another example of an opener is someone saying to you, 'But that was last year. Things are different now.' You could ignore that last comment and carry on with the conversation or you could stop it and say, 'What do you mean, different?' Even if you don't recognise the opener until you mull the conversation at a later time, you could bring it up next time you see the person: 'I was remembering our conversation and something you said puzzled me. What did you mean when you said . . .?'

Some people are nervous about picking up on openers because they feel they will be rejected if they try to find out more or feel that it is forbidden territory, or they may fear that the other person will think they are prying or that they have no right to ask. But if this were so, she would probably never have given the opener in the first place. Usually people give openers in the hope that they will be asked to enlarge on them to become more intimate and receive sympathy and emotional support. Don't let these opportunities pass you by: you may be glad of increased intimacy when you need support. Ignoring these cues shows that you are not interested in the other person. It can also indicate that you don't care.

*Watch for inconsistencies.* If a person says one thing but displays body language to suggest the opposite, say, for example, 'You say you don't care about it, but you look as though your world's fallen apart.' If a person says something that conflicts with what was said before say, for example, 'Now you just said . . . but last week you said that . . . I find that confusing.'

*Ask for specifics* if the other person is vague. For example, if he says that he's always left out of family discussions, ask for instances when this occurred. Giving examples helps clarify it in his mind and shows whether the general statement he made is accurate. If it is accurate, by understanding each situation you might be able to suggest a completely different interpretation from the one he'd given, or you may be able to spot what has happened in his behaviour to make others behave like that towards him, or how he can redress the balance by challenging the people concerned.

*Ask hypothetical questions* such as, 'What would happen if you . . .?' or, 'If you'd done that, how do you think he'd have reacted?' so that you understand the dynamics of the other person's relationships and explore the feasibility of various options.

*Focus on the problem* once you have explored the area in general terms. There may be more than one issue, but once you have the whole picture pick on one issue only to talk about and stick to that. If the conversation starts diverging, bring it back to the same issue: you can follow up another issue later.

*Allow silences*: they are OK and give time for you and the other person to think. He is more likely to enlarge on what he's been saying if there are silences inviting him to speak.

*Be aware of your voice.* Questions have to be asked in the right way, with the right tone of voice, with the right volume – loud enough to be heard, but not too loud as to make the other person fear her secrets will be overheard. Show sensitivity in the way you ask the questions and be ready to take the hint if you have overstepped the mark. Even if the other person doesn't want to tell you about it this time, by backing off you give her the confidence to confide at a later date, as she will see that you respect her and her needs.

*Develop rapport* by playing down differences between you, such as in upbringing and education, and don't use unfamiliar words or jargon: you are not meant to impress the other person but make communication between you as clear as possible.

Mirroring the other person's body language also develops rapport: if, for example, he sits cross-legged on the floor, to make you 'equal' sit in the same position too; if he sits slumped to one side in an armchair, you could do the same; if he pauses to take a drink, you could use the same opportunity to have a sip from yours. But don't mirror negative body language such as sitting huddled with folded arms – instead have a relaxed posture in the hope he will unconsciously mirror you. (Also see *Body language and social success* in Chapter 8, page 94.)

*Be gentle in your listening*: don't interrogate. Try to make the situation seem natural by not overplaying your temporary superiority because you are the one giving the help: don't fire question after question while getting only monosyllabic replies. Take it more steadily, without asking several questions together.

*Avoid telling the person what to do*: remember that what might be OK for you is not necessarily OK for another person. Explore possibilities and make suggestions, but the final decision should be hers.

## What can I say?

There are times when someone says something to you or divulges a confidence and you don't know what to say or how to react. Below are some examples of awkward situations you might find yourself in and suggested responses, which you can tailor to suit the person concerned, and the knowledge you have of that person and the situation:

*She tried to kill herself*. 'You must have been feeling very desperate to try to kill yourself. What's gone wrong . . .? Have you felt this bad before . . .? Did you mean to succeed or was it a cry for help . . .? How do you feel now . . .? Has anything changed for the better?'

*His son killed himself.* 'I'm so sorry to hear about your son. You must be completely and utterly devastated. It's one of a parent's worst nightmares . . . Do you know why he did it . . .? Had you any idea he felt this bad . . .? Can I do anything to help?'

*Her baby has just died.* 'It must be heartbreaking to lose a baby. I'm very sorry it's happened to you, you must be feeling dreadful. How did it happen . . .? When's the funeral . . .? Can I do anything to help?'

*She has had a miscarriage.* 'I'm terribly sorry you lost your baby. How many weeks were you . . .? (The age of the foetus is significant. If the foetus is legally viable, the parents can register the birth and death, and have a burial ceremony. They will also know what sex the baby was.) How awful for you. I am so sorry. How is your partner taking it? Are you able to talk about it . . .? Can I do anything to help?'

*He is separated or divorced.* 'I'm so sorry your marriage has broken down. I've heard the trauma involved is similar to bereavement. It must be a great strain for you . . . How are the children taking it? (If there are any.) How are you coping . . .? Is your family supportive . . .? Can I do anything to help?'

*He is bereaved.* 'I am so sorry you've lost . . . Was it very sudden? You must miss her very much . . . Grief for someone very close is one of the most stressful things that can happen to a person . . . Can I do anything to help . . .? When's the funeral?'

*She has been made redundant.* 'I am so sorry you've been made redundant. Did they give you much warning . . .? What are you going to do now . . .? What's the job market like at the moment in your field . . .? How long have you got before your wages stop . . .? Will you be able to manage?'

*He was sacked from his job.* 'I am so sorry you've lost your job. What happened . . .? Can you go to a tribunal on grounds of unfair dismissal . . .? How will you manage . . .? Will you be given a reference . . .? Have you consulted your union . . .? What are you going to do . . .? Is there anything I can do to help?'

*He has a child with Special Needs.* 'Tell me about your child's condition as I'd like to understand it and how you both deal with it . . . How can I be helpful towards him . . .? What shouldn't I say or do . . .? Is there anything I can do to help him?'

*She is mentally ill.* 'What's the matter . . .? What things make it worse . . .? What things help . . .? How can I help you . . .? Thank you for telling me. I'm glad you trust me enough to let me know.'

*He was imprisoned.* 'What happened . . .? Were you in for long . . .? What was it like . . .? What are you going to do now . . .? How has the experience changed you . . .? Has it been a problem finding work?'

*She is unemployed.* 'I'm sorry you're out of work. What was your last job . . .? What happened . . .? What are you looking for now . . .? Is there much demand . . .? Could you try for something a bit different? You might have better luck there . . . How do you spend your time . . .? Are your family and friends supportive?'

*He has been caught shoplifting.* 'What's going to happen . . .? How did you get caught . . .? Did you mean to do it or was it an accident . . .? Would you like me to come with you to court if you have to go?'

*She has an eating disorder.* 'What sort of eating disorder do you have . . .? How long have you had it . . .? What triggered the start of it . . .? Does anyone else know . . .? Have you tried to get help . . .? There is an eating disorder association that might be able to help you . . . Is your family understanding . . .? You must be feeling bad over this. Is there anything I can do to help?'

*He is an illegal drug user.* 'What drugs are you taking . . .? How long have you been taking them . . .? Have

you tried to stop . . .? Do you want to stop . . .? There are
organisations that can help . . . Does your family
know . . .? They could help support you through this if
you told them . . . Your doctor would be able to suggest
help for you . . .' (This one definitely needs specialised help
so you cannot take the entire burden of knowledge on
yourself. You need to persuade the user to get appropriate
help.)

*She wants to have her pregnancy terminated.* 'Why do
you want a termination . . .? What does the father
think . . .? How do you feel about this . . .? Does your
family know . . .? Do you know how to go about getting
an appointment? They always offer counselling before you
make the final decision . . . Would you like me to come
with you?' (If you feel that you cannot condone having a
pregnancy terminated for whatever reason, you must not
get into conversation with the person but tell her that she
must talk to someone else about it. Giving non-judgmental
help does not include moralising or making the person feel
worse than she already does.)

*He has been sexually abused as a child.* 'I'm so sorry.
That's terrible. Did you get help or tell anyone . . .? How is
it affecting your life now . . .? It sounds as though you
need professional help . . .'

*She is homosexual.* 'How long have you known . . .?
How do you feel about being homosexual . . .? Does your
family know . . .? Have you 'come out'...? Are you in a
homosexual relationship now . . .? Can I help in any way?'

*His home was burned down.* 'I'm so sorry. How awful for
you. Was anyone hurt . . .? Did you manage to save anything . . .? Was it insured . . .? Where are you living
now . . .? How are you managing . . .? Is there anything I
can do to help?'

*She has just been diagnosed with a terminal illness.* 'I'm
extremely sorry to hear that. What's wrong with you . . .?
How long have you got . . .? I feel stunned by the news, so

you must be in complete shock. How are you feeling . . .? Are you in pain . . .? How has your family taken it . . .? Can I do anything to help?'

Very often, when you offer help to someone in trouble, you know there isn't usually anything you can do, but it is important to make the offer – but only if you genuinely are prepared to help – so that the other person feels he has an ally in you and that he can come back to you again if things get worse or don't improve. Sometimes, the offer of practical help is needed but the person in need doesn't like to ask. For example, if a family is bereaved or has had a big shock, meals are one of the things that don't happen. An offer of cooking a pot of something to take round or to have the children over so that they can have some normality might be greatly appreciated.

It is often a big step for someone to unburden himself to another person, so thank him for trusting you enough to confide in.

# 8

# BODY LANGUAGE

The body language considered in this chapter is from the Western point of view – for body language differences in some other cultures see Chapter 20.

Body language accounts for over ninety per cent of information communicated in any face-to-face interaction, and you communicate even when you are silent. Information can be given away consciously, such as smiling at someone because you are pleased to see her, but most of your body language is subconscious: you are unaware of your expressions and gestures and so have no control over them. They give you away if you tell a lie or if you pretend to like something you really hate. Only very skilled and practised people can give *false* information through body language – for negative reasons such as lying to the police or conning someone to buy a product that does not live up to the description they give. Others can use controlled body language for positive purposes such as tempering their true feelings to retain a friendship, helping their counselling skills, backing up assertive comments by showing they mean what they say, and deliberately showing how they feel – in the hope that their love is guessed at and verbally returned.

## Learning body language

By watching parents' or carers' faces as a baby and young child, you learned to interpret facial expressions and copy them to show your own feelings. The rest of body language was learned in a similar way: by watching changes in body movements and hearing voice differences in people in a variety of situations. As a socially skilled adult, you are expected to be very familiar with all body language nuances, interpreting fine differences in expression, noticing the slight gestures people make and how their voices sound.

But some people do not pick up on the finer points of body language interpretation, and are not very skilled at showing the right emotions. This could be because their main carer was unskilled at showing different emotions or because she deliberately hid them, wanting to 'spare' them, or protect them from the more disturbing emotions such as fear, grief and anger. Other people are simply not equipped to notice body language because of a particular problem they have (as with autism spectrum disorders or learning difficulties) and so it largely passes them by. However, body language can be learnt at any age in a more formal way to make up for any lapses.

**Aggressive body language**
Signs of aggression can make people shy away from you especially if they do not feel comfortable or safe in your presence or if you are very unpredictable: kind and sweet one moment and nasty the next. People may find it hard to trust you or may find you unapproachable, which would interfere with your personal relationships and how successful you are at work – this is very important if you have customers to deal with. Aggressive body language includes elements of the following:

*Body*
- Erect posture: legs apart, a straight back, leaning forward (threateningly), standing rigidly.
- Pointing fingers, clenching fists, poking.

- Hands on hips or folded arms.
- Standing while the other person sits (making the most of your body size).
- Standing too close.

*Face*
- Constant unrelieved eye contact, half-closed eyes (threatening or angry).
- Jaw clenched, jaw jutting out.
- Pursed lips.
- Scowl.

*Voice*
- Shouting, accusing. ('You . . .')
- Sarcastic, condescending, patronising, sneering.
- Hard and unrelenting.

To avoid aggressive behaviour count to five or ten before making a response to something you don't like or gain time to control your feelings by asking the person to explain what she meant by what she said or did. Try to understand her point of view and then explain yours. Ask yourself if you are over-reacting and, if you are, apologise. Learn from your mistakes so that in time your aggression becomes more and more controlled and never resort to violence.

**Passive body language**
Showing signs of passivity leaves you vulnerable to being bullied or victimised as it suggests you are weak and unable to stand up for yourself, making you an ideal target. Passive body language includes elements of the following:

*Body*
- Poor posture: a hunched back, rounded shoulders, head down, arms folded.
- Retreating or moving away from the other person.

- Biting nails and skin around the nails.
- Picking at clothes.
- Wringing hands together.
- Covering your mouth.

*Face*
- Little eye contact: eyes keep looking at the floor.
- Looking nervous or frightened.
- Trembling lips.
- Worried frown.
- Flinching (from an imagined threat).
- Looking over-apologetic (big 'cow' eyes, furrowed brow).

*Voice*
- Mumbling: soft voice and indistinct words.
- Stuttering: getting stuck on one syllable or sound in the word and finding it hard to complete the word.
- Verbal stumbling: words running into each other, mispronounced words, leaving off endings.
- Tremor in your voice, hesitations, long pauses.
- Much coughing and clearing of your throat.

To avoid victimisation learn assertive body language – described below – and monitor whether you are using it. Prepare yourself in advance for encounters with difficult people by practising standing and speaking assertively. Visualise yourself as an assertive person. Learn your rights and how to defend them, and how to say no (see Chapter 10). And learn to protect yourself from put-downs (see Chapters 17 and 18).

**Assertive body language**
Assertive body language is welcoming and interested, and encourages people to trust you and respect your judgment. It includes elements of the following:

*Body*
- Erect posture, a straight back.
- If standing: legs apart, hands by your sides.
- Facing people squarely.
- Head up.
- Standing or sitting at a comfortable distance. (You should adapt to the culture you are in: in some cultures people expect to stand or sit extremely close – see Chapter 20.)
- Crouching to talk to a young child or someone sitting down so that your eyes are at the same level and the other person does not have to strain her neck to look at you.
- Relaxed.

*Face*
- Full eye contact with occasional breaking away.
- Expression mirroring what you are saying.
- Smiling openly to invite conversation.

*Voice*
- Words spoken clearly and firmly.
- Even, well-modulated tone (expressively going up and down rather than in a boring monotone).
- Confident.
- Relaxed, not edgy or tight.

To assertively show you dislike someone using body language: keep your distance, don't smile, answer questions economically – using as few words as possible – don't laugh at his jokes and keep eye contact brief. To assertively show you like someone using body language: be physically near, smile, answer questions fully and ask some of your own, volunteer information, laugh at her jokes and maintain frequent eye contact.

### Knowing how much to show

As a socially skilled adult, you need to be aware of your body language to tone it down when necessary or even hide how you feel about something. The examples below illustrate inappropriate adult body language: the descriptions are more suited to the body language of a young child.

- You are given a present that you don't like and you let the disappointment show on your face.

- You are desperate for the toilet so cross your legs and jump up and down while holding your crotch.

- You are excited about going somewhere and, in front of all your colleagues, you jump up and down unable to contain your glee.

- You 'wear your heart on your sleeve', by showing everyone whom you adore – before you have any knowledge about how this person feels towards you. Here you are laying yourself open to embarrassment and ridicule, a target for teasing.

Your body language often determines how well others respond to you. If you are unskilful at showing your positive feelings (such as by not looking pleased to see someone when you are) and don't manage to hide your negative feelings (such as by taking a step back when someone you don't like approaches you), you risk offence. This does not, however, apply to situations where it is important for you to display negative emotions such as when someone is unwelcome in trying to chat you up. Then you are at liberty to make your feelings clear, with the level of offence appropriate to the level of nuisance and, if the level of offence is great, you can walk away or leave.

Other times you might not want people to know how you really feel include when you are lying – you might want to avoid unnecessarily hurting someone's feelings; when you have a surprise in store; or when you are disappointed that the person you love has not come to the party after all.

### Body language and social success

In being socially successful, you need to be careful to deliver the correct – expected or hoped for – response to something, both in words and in body language. If you don't match your body language with what you say you can sometimes give conflicting messages and either the receiver will be confused or will misinterpret your meaning. For example, it is no good to say at an interview, 'Yes, I would take the job if it were offered to me' if your voice hesitates or wavers and you glance away from your interviewer whilst saying it, tightly wringing your hands together. Despite your words, it would look as though you weren't at all sure whether you'd take the job.

To show interest in what someone is saying, you should lean forward, nod your head, make frequent eye contact and appropriate noises such as 'Hmm', 'Ah' and 'I see'. If the person says something you don't like, you can jerk your head slightly back or use silence to show disapproval if you can't think how to verbalise it.

An erect posture commands respect and helps you to be taken seriously. If you fold your arms, you create a barrier between you and the other person so only use this posture when you want to put emotional distance between you. Fiddling and twiddling with possessions or your clothes are signs of nervousness and feeling uncomfortable: try to look relaxed and at ease with your company and surroundings.

If you want to start talking to someone you move closer, and when you wish to finish the conversation, but find it hard to, edging away lets the other person know that it's time to steer it to a close. (Also see Chapter 5.) If you are very friendly with another person or feel in accord with him, your body language might match his: when he crosses his legs you might cross yours, if he leans back and stretches out an arm you might do the same. This synchronisation of your bodies brings you emotionally closer and aids disclosure. (Also see *Listening skills that help achieve intimacy* in Chapter 7, page 80.)

Practise postures and expressions in the mirror and listen to yourself on tape while verbally acting out a variety of scenarios and check whether the sound of your voice matches what you say. Whenever possible, over anything that is important, decide how you want to look beforehand. For example, use the advance warning of an interview – or date – to imagine how you want to appear to your interviewers – or date – and what behaviour you must display to achieve this.

### Personal body space

You will have your own idea about what is comfortable for you regarding how close you sit, or stand near to, another person. Much of it largely depends on your personality: if you are relaxed, happy and outgoing, you are more likely to be comfortable sitting or standing much closer to someone you barely know than a passive person who is tense, anxious and fears meeting new people.

Personal body space can be considered to have three zones: for intimate distances you can feel the other person's breath on you and your bodies may touch; for social distances you stand or sit close enough to be easily heard such as at a drinks party, and for public distances you have to project your voice to be heard such as when you are addressing an audience. Your personal body space varies because of who you are, whom you are with, the circumstances and your culture (see Chapter 20) – if someone invades the body space you need to feel comfortable with that person, you will want to move away. Generally, the more you like someone, the closer you stand and the more you touch. And for those you like less, or know less, the converse is true, but there are some situations where your usual body distance from a person might decrease. For example:

- If you are very angry with someone, you might stand closer to him than normal to use your proximity as a threatening gesture.
- If you have fallen in love with someone and she has told you she feels the same, you will sit much closer.
- If you experience a tragedy such as bereavement you need comforting so will accept friends being very close to you. This physical proximity may revert to normality after the crisis is over or you may have developed comfort from this new level of intimacy and wish to carry on being physically closer.
- If you board at college your friendships are likely to be much more intimate than they had been when you were at a day school. Having to get all your physical comfort and support from your friends as your parents and siblings are not with you, you are much more likely to sit nearer and touch more often.
- If you are lonely, you may well tolerate, and be comforted by, physical proximity.
- If you are travelling on crowded public transport you will tolerate being pushed close to a stranger for the sake of needing to reach your destination.

### People watching

You can learn more about body language by watching people, whether in public or on television. Watch people's expressions, note their gestures and listen to their voices. The following examples only give suggested body language when observing members of the public. Just because a suggestion has been made, it doesn't mean it happens every time. Make your own observations.

An angry parent has a harsh, suppressed shout – as he's in public he will probably hold back, and he sounds threatening ('I'm warning you . . .'). He will draw his eyebrows into a frown, have a sneering or pursed mouth and have half shut eyes. He drags his children along by their arms, squeezing them tightly. When his hands are free, his fists will be clenched and he may wag a pointing finger warningly.

When someone is lying he has a red face, cannot meet the other person's gaze squarely and keeps dropping his gaze downwards. His fingers twiddle awkwardly with keys, hair or items of clothing and he keeps touching his face with light strokes. His feet keep bending upwards and his body looks tense.

**Correct interpretation of body language**
Some body language is used for more than one message and it is up to you to interpret the composite of all the different little messages in the context of what's been said and by whom. For example, a man is embarrassed by the details a woman has gone into about her sex life. He blushes, lowers his gaze, twiddles with his clothes and bends his feet upwards. These are all body language messages for lying. But in the context of the situation, he couldn't have just lied because he didn't say anything. And the other person hadn't accused him of lying because she was busy talking about herself. So the correct interpretation must be that of embarrassment.

Body language is a complex system of messages that need to be taken in their entirety to interpret them correctly. But sometimes you do not have sufficient information to make an assessment, such as when someone has written you a letter or email: you can neither see what his body is doing nor interpret the tone of his voice. Lack of body message also occurs when speaking over the telephone or if you are severely visually impaired: you only have the voice to go on. For a profoundly deaf person, you may be able to lip-read or read sign language, but you would miss out on the fine nuances of the voice and may be unable to tell which words are emphasised.

## Mood and body language

Body language can be used to communicate mood. For example, speaking in a flat, uninterested voice suggests you feel low; a loud, high-pitched, fast voice suggests you feel happy or excited. Other people noticing your mood will change how they respond to you. For example, if you give a very happy laugh over something funny, the other person is likely to join in, catching your mood. But if you only give a very weak smile, the other person is not likely to respond at all, feeling totally damped and not sympathetically disposed towards you.

Other examples of positive mood body language are: a firm handshake, a warm smile, a sparkle in your eyes as you smile, an affectionate hug, a welcoming tone of voice, laughing readily at funny moments or jokes and warm comments about the other person. All these things help people to like you and find being with you a rewarding experience: try to transmit messages that are beneficial to your goals and relationships.

## Word emphasis

Word emphasis can change the entire meaning of a sentence. For example, saying, 'I will go to work today' without any particular emphasis suggests the speaker is simply imparting information. But if different words are emphasised, the expression is not a statement but: defiance ('I *will* go to work today'), or a confirmation of someone's destination ('I will go to *work* today'), or a confirmation of time ('I will go to work *today*'). It could also be a confirmation of who will be going to work ('*I* will go to work today').

Note which words are emphasised in other people's

speech and remember to give the correct emphases when you speak.

### Misuse of body language

It is not a misuse of body language to pretend to like a gift when you don't, just to be polite; here your motive is to avoid hurting the other person's feelings. But using body language to pretend a feeling you don't have to further your own ends, such as persuading someone to go to bed with you, or to gain confidences to use the information for your own ends, is an abuse of the skill. If you are caught misusing skills you will be instantly disliked and lose respect others may have had for you. You can also lose friends.

# 9

# COMPLIMENTS

Compliments are gratifying comments on how you are doing or how you look that encourage you to do more of the same and to reward the person who complimented you by showing pleasure. Similarly, when you bestow a compliment on someone else, you please him and will receive the reward of observing his delight if he is sufficiently skilled to show it.

### Receiving compliments skilfully

*Be courteous.* If you have been brought up to be modest you might reject a compliment, denying it has any meaning for you, or believe you don't deserve it. Suppose someone tells you that you have good taste in clothes; you might reply, 'Oh, I don't. It's probably luck that things go so well together.' To you, this may seem like a polite and modest response, but it is actually rude: you have rejected the compliment, returning it as an unwanted gift and there is a possibility the other person won't want to compliment you in the future. A simple 'Thank you' is better.

*Reward the person who compliments you* by showing him what his words have meant to you. By doing this you are not only saying a worthier thank you but are also encouraging him to compliment you in the future giving you both further opportunities of getting reward and feeling good about yourselves.

For example, if your colleague at work tells you that the layout of your report is much clearer and easier to understand than the old format, you could say, 'Thank you. I'm so pleased you think so. I now feel more comfortable about presenting it to the boss.' If someone tells you that you are a very careful driver and that she feels safe when she's in the car with you, you could say, 'That's very kind of you. I do feel responsible for my passengers, so I try very hard to concentrate and drive sensibly. I'm glad you appreciate it.' If a friend admires the painting you've just finished, telling you that it looks very realistic and that you've obviously got talent, you could reply, 'Thanks. I was a bit worried that it was too simplistic. I'm glad you like it.'

*Clarify the compliment* by asking for a vague message to be made clearer so that you can fully appreciate the value of what has been said. Suppose someone tells you that you are very good with children. Does she mean you are patient? Are good at listening to them? Enjoy playing with them? Telling them jokes? Are affectionate towards them? Is this based on a single observation or over a period of time? Are you good with anyone's children or just your nephew?

So you need to ask, 'What makes you think so?' She might say, 'I saw you comfort your nephew when he fell over. You were very gentle with him and he soon lost his fear of his blooded knee. I was touched.' Then you can comment on a fully understood compliment: 'Yes, I think you're right. I'd never thought about it before. I certainly love my nephew and would like children of my own some day. It was kind of you to point it out.'

*Separate the compliment from the underlying purpose* so that you have less risk of unnecessarily offending the person who gave it. For example, your partner wants to buy you a fleece jumper but the one he says suits you extremely well is one he's already chosen for himself but in a different colour: he wants to buy them both. You could say, 'Thank you, I like it on me too, but I'd prefer to have one completely different from yours. I'd feel uncomfortable being together, wearing similar clothes. I want to have a separate identity.' Here, the underlying purpose is your partner wanting to buy you the fleece. You can accept the compliment about the fleece suiting you; having the same fleece as him is a separate issue.

If someone tells you how much she admires you and has come to love you, don't say, 'Don't be ridiculous' as this implies she is stupid and is a put-down. Instead, concentrate instead on *why* she said it. If you do not want her loving attention, say so gracefully: 'I feel flattered that you admire me and touched that you love me. But I'm afraid that, although I am fond of you, I do not love you.' Here, the underlying purpose was that the woman wanted to know if you returned her love. So you accepted her declaration of love as a compliment and then concentrated on gently telling her what she needed to know.

*Accept thanks with grace.* When someone says to you, 'Thank you for helping, it was very kind of you', you should say something like, 'I was glad to do it' or, 'I enjoyed it' rather than, 'Well, you have to do your bit', which tells the other person that you hadn't wanted to help out at all and only did it because you felt it was your duty. Even if this is how you feel, it is impolite to let him know. He will probably avoid asking your help in the future, or put you on his last resort list. It is a compliment if others call on you for help when they are in a crisis – this is not referring to people taking advantage of you, but the normal give and take a friendship would create – and you need to acknowledge it.

### Giving compliments skilfully

*Be confident* when you compliment: feeling awkward and self-conscious or worrying about how much your compliment will be valued makes you deliver it in an inhibited and unrewarding way. Concentrate on what you have to say, not on how you feel. Mumbling so that you can't be heard only increases your embarrassment and makes the other person feel discomfited, as he will have to ask you to repeat what you've just said.

*Remember things you like to hear* and try to match these with what you say. For example, if you are intensely interested in clothes and you compliment a friend on his clothing, he will know that the compliment is genuinely meant – you wouldn't say something about clothes you didn't mean.

*Remember things the other person likes to hear*: if you know about concerns of hers, you can say things that will help put her mind at rest, but for this to work, everything you say must be genuinely meant. Flattery is easily detected and instils distrust.

*Be specific* when you give a compliment so that the other person understands exactly what it is you like. For example, if your friend has a new hairstyle don't say, 'I like your haircut' but, 'The shorter style is more flattering to your face.'

*Non-compliments* are ungraceful and ungenerous, leaving the receiver puzzled as to what it is you wanted to say. Suppose your group of friends is taking it in turns to cook for each other. Your friend Martin has just cooked dinner and you are the only one of the group who has not yet shown off his culinary skills. You are worried about what the others will think of your meal when it comes to your turn to cook. Saying, 'It looks as though all of you are really good cooks' is a non-compliment: when you are eating food that has been cooked for you, you must aim the compliment at the person who cooked it rather than firing a general statement encompassing him and all your mutual friends. Instead say, 'This tastes wonderful. You're a great cook, Martin.'

Another way of giving a non-compliment is to put

yourself down. If you are going to compliment, do it wholeheartedly without first considering how the person measures up to you. A compliment should be absolute. If the person deserves it, say it. For example, Mandy has just knitted herself a jumper and it looks great. Saying, 'I could never do that' is a non-compliment. Instead say, 'That looks fantastic, Mandy. You're so clever not only to have made a jumper but also to have done such a great job. And the colours you've chosen blend very well. You must be so proud of it.'

*Choose the right moment.* When giving a compliment, you need to choose the right moment so that what you say can be fully appreciated. For example, when someone is ill with flu she doesn't want to hear how pretty she looks. Or if she is late, she doesn't want to hear about how well organised she is – unless it's to damp down a criticism by first saying she is usually very organised and punctual. Or someone about to enter a board-room meeting to present a proposal of marketing for a new product will not want to be reminded of how well he'd performed as a clown at your niece's birthday party: a glimpse of juvenile behaviour in his private life may adversely affect colleagues' view of him in what is a very serious and purposeful setting. So wait until you are alone together in an informal environment before you tell him what a great clown he made.

*Make sure the compliment is not past its use-by date.* Compliments are best said at the time to add meaning to the situation and to show you've been paying attention to what's been going on. For example, a compliment about your friend's singing at a karaoke night is best given as soon as she has finished, not a month later: she would wonder why, if you really meant it, you hadn't said it at the time. Are you so mean and grudging with your compliments that you have to weigh it up for four weeks before you allow it to a person?

Telling someone she threw a great party a year ago is

rather past its date. But you could repeat a compliment you said in the past and bring it up-to-date by saying: 'I so loved the party you gave last year. Might you throw another?'

*Don't go over-the-top*: ensure the level of praise you give represents the worth of the thing you are praising. If you under-praise something, you are not rewarding the person enough; but over-praising can be equally offending: it makes it very hard for the compliment to be accepted when the person *knows* – and is not just being modest – that she does not deserve this over-the-top attention.

For example, it would be inappropriate to say, 'That was fantastic. Absolutely fantastic. Unbelievable', when you're talking about a simple sponge cake your friend made – unless he has a disability which makes the baking of a cake a real achievement – but even for the average person's first time at baking, your response should be little more than: 'It looks and tastes great. Well done', otherwise it can be interpreted as a put-down, with you being patronising rather than genuine.

Another risk is that, if you over-praise something, you have no higher praise to offer a worthier cause so must use the same words you have already used for that lesser cause, which belittles the more deserving cases.

*Be genuine*: false praise rarely fools anyone. If someone deserves to be complimented give the praise freely; don't sour it. For example, if you say to someone, 'I'm so glad to see you looking so much better *these days*', it implies she used to look dreadful. This may well be interpreted as a snide comment rather than a compliment. Instead, you could say, 'You look really well.' There are no unkind hidden messages here; it is a 'clean' compliment that has to be taken at face value.

### Witnessing compliments

By interfering with compliments other people receive you can end up undoing them, which will make people regard you as mean-spirited, jealous and socially unskilled. For example, when Harriet lavishly compliments Rakshika in your company, you might rudely say to Rakshika, 'I bet your head won't fit through the door now it's so big', implying Rakshika does not deserve the compliment and belittling what Harriet has said, making her feel uncomfortable. Either keep quiet or say something nice such as, 'I didn't realise you could do all those things. That's fantastic. Well done' or, 'You must be proud of your achievements.'

Another way to belittle Harriet for praising Rakshika would be to say, 'And what do you want from her?' implying that Harriet only said those things because she wanted a favour from Rakshika. Although in some circumstances this scenario could be used to tease, the difference is the people involved will know you are bantering because of your friendship with them, the warmth in your voice and the smile on your face as you say it.

It is also possible to undo a compliment of your own by unskilful handling post-compliment by, for example, aggressively saying, 'I hope you're going to cut the ends off those things' after taking someone a bunch of flowers for her birthday. This suggests she is incompetent and does not sufficiently value your gift. If you feel you needed to mention the stem ends you could gently say, 'Do you know that the flowers last longer if you cut off the ends?'

# 10

# ASSERTION

Assertion is dealing openly and honestly with others while showing respect by not putting them down or being judgmental. It is a middle ground between aggression and non-assertion (passivity) and, for many, it can be extremely hard to achieve. To appreciate fully what assertion is, what it isn't must also be looked at.

### Aggression

Aggressive people go all out for what they want and don't care who gets in their way: anyone obstructing them from their goal gets emotionally trampled on. Words to describe aggressive people include: accusing, arrogant, bellicose, belligerent, bigoted, blaming, bossy, controlling, cruel, demanding, dictatorial, domineering, egotistical, a gossip, grumpy, having a short fuse, hostile, impatient, imperious, intolerant, irritable, lordly, manipulative, a megalomaniac, moody, moralising, a nag, narrow-minded, offensive, rude, a saboteur, sarcastic, sly, superior, tactless, and uncompromising.

Some ways of being aggressive are obvious such as throwing a tantrum or fighting someone; others, which are subtler – and are in the passive-aggressive category – will be looked at later.

*Making accusations* such as by saying, 'You're rude';

'You think you're so clever'; 'You hate to be wrong' is aggressive: try to avoid starting sentences with 'You . . .' Instead, you could say, 'That wasn't very polite'; 'That wasn't one of your better jokes'; 'That's not the way I see it.'

Even if you think an aggressive comment is well deserved, think carefully about how this will affect your relationships in the long run – building hostility might not matter for a complete stranger you never have to see again, but could make life harder for you at work, or socially. We all make mistakes; instead try to concentrate on how they can be put right – after, if you like, telling the other person what she's done wrong, how it has affected you and how you feel about it. Just don't accuse.

*Showing anger* is only considered assertive if the amount shown is appropriate to the situation and the need for displaying anger is clear. For example, it would be strange not to show anger when your partner informs you he has been having an affair or has gambled away your holiday money, but shouting or throwing tantrums when someone has made a simple mistake such as forgetting to call you to say she'll be late home for supper is plainly inappropriate and aggressive.

*Giving put-downs* is making someone feel bad about himself – or making him feel small (see Chapter 17). They can be a direct insult, or subtler: 'I'm surprised that fits you so well' or, 'I expect even you can manage that.'

*Being sexist or racist* (see Chapter 18) is putting someone down because of a difference in sex, race or culture to you and shows prejudice, ignorance and lack of general life education.

*Giving orders* does not make people respond positively. For example, saying, 'You should have done as you were told' or, 'Go away' or, 'You must get it now' may encourage the person you were addressing to respond to the aggression rather than your request.

*Saying things to punish* such as, 'I'm never going to speak to you again' or, 'You can go on your own then' makes you lose out as well as the person you're addressing if you carry out your threat – and if you don't carry it out, people won't take what you say seriously, and you lose face. So, with this sort of punishment, neither of you has truly 'won' (see Chapter 12 for help on dealing with conflict). An assertive approach would be to say: 'That was very unkind of you and I don't respect you for it' or, 'I don't think you had to talk to me like that to get your point across.'

### Passive-aggression

When you are being passive-aggressive, you don't openly fight back or become nasty, preferring non-confrontational methods: you like to treat the other person badly behind his back or in such a way that you hope he won't know how to protect himself. This type of aggression is harder for the other person to deal with because it is carried out covertly or in such a way that he is very unsure how to respond.

*Being bigoted* is being set in your ways: being intolerant of others and having beliefs you rigidly stick to despite evidence to the contrary. Saying for example, 'What can you expect from a single parent?' is hard for that single parent to challenge and, as shown through Alys and Dave's conversations in Chapter 6, attempting to change viewpoints of people with set attitudes is often not worth the bother.

*Controlling* other people, so that they do what you want for no good reason apart from pandering to your whim, is bullying. Ask yourself if you are being reasonable, logical and respectful in your handling of other people if you are prone to controlling them.

*Giving grudging compliments* by saying something like, 'I suppose this is your way of saying sorry' or, 'I suppose for you that was very good' is aggressive (also see Chapter 9). Compliments should be generous and genuine: 'If you're doing this to say sorry, then thank you' or, 'Well done. I know you find this sort of thing hard.'

*Being tactless* on a regular basis suggests you don't care whom you hurt or how often. Consider the appropriateness of your comment before saying it or recall whether you have made a similar mistake before; note how others put similar questions or comments to that person. Are you on the same level of intimacy as they are? Or is that particular subject not appropriate for you to bring up in the same way?

*Manipulating* someone is dishonestly persuading her to do something for you such as pretending to like her and enjoy her company, when in reality you are only tolerating her because you want a lift, a favour or a mention in her will: you have a hidden agenda of your own to further your needs.

*Moralising* is meaningless if you have never had the same temptations or opportunities as the person you've just been criticising. Any judgmental attitude – unless it is universally accepted as the norm – is aggressive.

*Sabotage* is ensuring that someone's plans go awry in a very underhand way. Examples include: accepting the responsibility of posting someone's job application form but tearing it up instead; deliberately introducing faults into something another person is building or designing, or deliberately spilling coffee over someone's drawings or artwork; and vastly reducing someone's chances of success in a relationship by stealing all the attention, or telling the prospective partner a few things about the other person – either true or untrue.

*Being sarcastic* is saying one thing while meaning the opposite, for example saying, 'Oh that was clever', just after someone has dropped something, or telling someone she looks smart when she's wearing a filthy boiler suit.

Sarcasm can be very witty; if it isn't used to hurt or offend it is not being aggressive. Saying to another waiting passenger on a platform, 'I see the train service is up to its usual high standards', when the train is very late neither hurts you nor the other passenger – and the large train company can bear the slight. The benefit of using sarcasm here is showing commonality with a fellow passenger and can be used as an opener to a longer conversation.

*Shunning* or ignoring someone is aggressive: if someone has offended you it is better to explain why to give her a chance to defend herself and to offer to make amends, or you risk never being on good terms again.

*Spreading gossip* is malicious especially when it is untrue and repeating any news given to you in confidence is spiteful. If you are found out, you will lose that person's trust. You may also lose the trust of the person to whom you divulge the information – unless, for example, to a well-known, well-chosen partner – as he's witnessed what you do with other people's confidences.

### Non-assertion or passivity

Passive people tend to prefer not to be noticed, always choose the easiest path at the time for a peaceful existence and avoid confrontation. Words to describe passive people include: afraid, apologetic, avoids or dreads social situations, can be made to change her mind, does not stand up for what she believes in, gives up easily, gives way, inferior, malleable, nervous, panicky, prefers not to be noticed, quiescent, sensitive, submissive, tongue-tied, unsure, victim, and a yes-person.

If you are non-assertive or passive you are shy and timid and tend to get emotionally trampled on by aggressive people. If you are very timid even other timid people might take advantage of you and you may find it very hard to protect yourself.

*Asking indirectly* for something is not likely to get you the same results or respect as a direct question would get (see Chapter 14). You might not even manage to ask at all, hoping that someone might guess your needs.

*Being over-apologetic* does not earn respect. You should only apologise when you have genuine reason to be sorry: it becomes meaningless if you use it in every other sentence. It also begs someone to victimise you or take advantage of you. If you are genuinely sorry about something and apologies are needed, saying sorry as though you mean it once or even twice is sufficient. More is over-kill and is likely to embarrass the other person.

*Giving and receiving compliments* unskilfully shows you up to be socially awkward as well as passive (also see Chapter 9). If, for example, someone says, 'This is great. You're a good cook' and you reply, 'No I'm not. I usually burn everything' the compliment falls flat. If you ignore opportunities for complimenting other people you will be seen as unappreciative. And if, when you try to compliment, you show embarrassment, the other person will also feel discomfited.

*Hesitant speech* shows that you are nervous and are expecting a negative outcome, especially if you are asking for something and you 'um' and 'er'. Being firm in the way you speak does not guarantee you get the answer you want but your request will be taken more seriously.

*Hoping it will go away* by keeping quiet and not doing anything to get noticed does not get results. Often it is better simply to confront the issue so that the problem gets aired, discussed and then resolved.

*Putting yourself down* is saying uncomplimentary things about yourself such as, 'I'm so clumsy' (see *Self put-downs* in Chapter 17, page 186). By putting yourself down you are not showing respect for yourself, so how can you expect others to?

### In reality

In reality, it is unlikely that someone is wholly an aggressive or passive person: you relate differently to different people and so your behaviour changes depending with whom you are dealing. For example, a girl who is bullied at home by her mother may be very timid when at home. But when she gets to college she may be aggressive, taking her anger and frustration out on the more passive students she comes across and does a bit of bullying herself. Or she may bully her own children and/or her partner. Someone who is loud and boisterous with his friends may be extremely shy and tongue-tied when introduced to a stranger at a party, away from his friendship group. A person who is bossy and domineering when with her family may seem sweet and gentle to the staff that look after her in the nursing home.

Both aggressive and passive people tend to have poor self-esteem. Often their behaviour stems from the bad feelings they have about themselves. In becoming assertive, you learn to change yourself for the better.

### Assertion

Assertive people get on with their life and are always moving forward: they know what they want and how to get there and do not do this at other people's expense. Words and phrases to describe an assertive person include: accepts responsibility for mistakes, authoritative, commanding, confident, fair, honest, in control, just, mature, non-judgmental, open, reasonable, relaxed, respected, socially adept, trustworthy, and what you see is what you get.

Assertion reaps rewards of having: high self-esteem, equal relationships, open and honest communication, others accept it when you say no, others respect you, a greater understanding of others and the skills to protect yourself from put-downs. Part of being assertive is also being socially adept – having the skills that are described in this book.

## Choosing when to behave assertively

By deliberately choosing not to assert your rights you are still being assertive because you remain in control of the situation. But it would cease being assertive behaviour if you were forced to do something, or you failed to do something, against your better judgment, because of pressure applied by another person.

*Choosing to be passive.* When you visit an elderly relative you need to be passive to stay no matter how bored you are. It would also be inappropriate to correct a prejudiced relative if he is too old to understand your up-to-date arguments or politically correct statements: there is little point in upsetting him, if no benefit would come about, by pointing anything out to him that would go against what he is used to.

Another good time to be passive is if you are being threatened with physical violence or are being mugged. For your own safety you should either cooperate or run away. You might also choose to behave passively because you want to be included in a group or not be expelled from a clique you are in. Or it may be that you are at a social function and do not wish your opposing views to be aired for fear of ridicule or of shocking others. Or you might deliberately choose to behave passively when, for example, you do not have the energy to pursue something further.

*Choosing to be aggressive.* If someone wrongly accuses you of spreading gossip round the office it would be in order for you to challenge him in front of the staff in the office to clear your name, and for you to demand an apology. You sometimes need to show your anger so that the other person understands how his actions have affected you.

If you see a child being bullied it would be appropriate

for you to get angry with the people who are doing the bullying to protect the child. It would also be appropriate, if you knew that someone was being falsely accused of stealing, for example, to stick up for her and get your voice heard.

*Choosing to be assertive.* If someone has upset you, you have good reason to discuss it with her so that she is less likely to repeat the offence and to save a relationship that you care about. You also need to be assertive to protect yourself from put-downs in all their guises (looked at in Chapters 17 and 18) and to show a confident, capable and trustworthy you.

### Personal rights

There are well-known personal rights that everyone is entitled to protect and uphold. If you do not recognise your rights and stand up for them, other people define your role for you (see Chapter 4) and you stop being yourself.

Gordon expects Abigail to do the bulk of the housework and childcare despite them both having full-time jobs. Abigail feels it is unfair that Gordon reads the evening newspaper while she cooks. To redress the balance she could say, 'Gordon, we are both out at work all day. I'm just as tired as you when we get in so I think we should split the household chores more fairly. Since I get in first it seems sensible that I shop for, and cook, the evening meal but I'd like you to take over helping the children with their homework and getting them ready for bed.'

Sometimes your right is unclear and you have to feel your way by negotiating with the other party. When it is Haroon's turn to clear up the communal kitchen in the house he shares with four other students he has a college deadline to meet and doesn't have time to do both. Although Haroon has a right to have time to do his work he also has an obligation to his responsibilities. To refuse to clean the kitchen outright is likely to lose the respect the others have for him and to antagonise them. It also shows a lack of respect for them, expecting them to take over his share. However, if he negotiates with one of them, explaining why he left his assignment to the last minute, he may be able to persuade her to swap her kitchen duty with his.

Commonly known personal rights are given below: if you are unsure at any time whether what you are doing or saying is valid, consult this list. If what you are doing upholds one or more of these rights you can have the confidence to go ahead knowing that your behaviour and expectations are reasonable.

1. I have the right to state my needs and prioritise them.
2. I have the right to be treated as an equal.
3. I have the right to some time alone and for privacy.
4. I have the right to make my own decisions and take responsibility for them.
5. I have the right to say yes and no to others and have my decision accepted.
6. I have the right to change my mind.
7. I have the right to ask for clarification without being made to feel small because I don't understand or know the answer.
8. I have the right to ask for what I want and understand that others have the right to refuse me.
9. I have the right to refuse responsibility for other people's problems.
10. I have the right to interact with others without changing my behaviour merely for their approval.
11. I have the right to be successful.
12. I have the right to change any part of me.

Being aware of your rights gives you the confidence to know when they have been violated so that you can take steps to protect them, which protects your self-esteem and makes you less emotionally vulnerable. However, you must recognise these rights are for everyone and respect other people's need to uphold theirs. For example, you might make what you see as a reasonable request, but the other person does have the right to say no and you must respect that without trying to make her change her mind.

There may be times when you choose to put your needs secondary to the needs of others and so deliberately choose not to protect your rights: this is still assertive behaviour because you have made a conscious decision to put your needs aside temporarily for a greater or more pressing need in someone else.

### Saying no

Sometimes you need to put your needs first and say no to other people's requests – such as when the price is too high or it is inconvenient. However, saying no can be difficult because you may fear being labelled mean or having your rejection of the request interpreted as a personal rejection. But if you say your piece assertively, this is less likely to happen.

When you say no, have an upright posture and face the other person squarely. Meet his gaze and look completely serious without the hint of a smile. Carefully pronounce all your words at a volume high enough to be heard, clearly emphasising the word no. Use the person's name to add further weight to your refusal. If you find these things hard to carry out, practise saying no to yourself in a mirror: check your expression is serious and ensure that your lips plainly show the word no as this will give a clearer message to the receiver that you mean what you say. Passive (such as slouching) or unclear (such as smiling) body language suggests you will easily buckle under pressure, encouraging the other person to badger you to change your mind.

The words you use when you say no are also important: you need to be firm and show respect for the other person. Suppose Janette, a married woman at work much older than you, harasses you by constantly flirting but then asks you out for a meal. You have no wish to go out with her or interfere with the relationship she has with her husband and children. You could say, aggressively, 'You must be joking!' Here you have just insulted her. You could say passively, 'No thanks, Janette, I've something on.' But you may have to say no again in the future, as you are only saying no for now.

If you say assertively, 'No thanks, Janette, I don't want to' you have not said anything offensive about her or to her, simply stating that you don't want to go. It would be up to Janette whether she pressed for a reason; in which case you must give it straight: you don't go out with married women. Do not say you don't fancy her, as she will be offended. This also implies the fact she is married with children would not stop you from starting an affair and she would be more likely to keep trying to make herself attractive to you.

Sometimes you cannot give an immediate answer: don't be afraid to ask for time to think it over and do listen to your inner feelings as gut instincts can often give you an answer when logic fails. Be clear in your own mind about what you want before you share it with the other person and, when you have decided, stick to it; be firm. It can help to practise what you are going to say in private, or to another person altogether, to give you confidence. Remember why it is important that you must occasionally say no – you have those rights to protect and there's no one else who can do it for you.

If you struggle for the words you need, use the other person's own words in your reply: 'No I don't want to . . .' If you feel the person deserves an explanation then give it but don't overdo your excuses. If necessary compromise and meet the person half way, or tell the person you are refusing just for now or give an alternative suggestion.

Sometimes there is no other option than to say no and leave it at that. For example, your son and daughter-in-law expect you to be available at all times to baby-sit your grandchildren. You resent this, feeling you are taken for granted. You are determined to refuse the next time you are asked so that they understand you do have a life of your own. You could say, 'No, Diane, I can't. I promised myself an evening out with Asha.' And, if you like, you could add, 'Don't forget I, too, have a social life.'

If a friend called Gary offers you some Ecstasy in the pub, you could just say, 'No thanks, Gary. I don't take drugs.' If a friend called Marte asks you to help her get signatures for a petition but you don't believe in the cause, you could say, 'No, Marte. I'm sorry I can't help but I have to believe in whatever I do.'

If you are invited to a dinner party with your partner and the person who issued the invitation is pressuring you for an immediate answer, you can say, 'It sounds lovely but I'll have to let you know since I don't know what Zolán's got planned.'

# 11

# RELATING TO OTHERS

When relating to other people, you need to communicate in a way that cannot be misunderstood, give specific rather than vague feedback, and show you are sensitive to the other person's needs. This chapter is concerned with avoiding pitfalls in unclear and insensitive communication.

**Communicating with non-native speakers and 'outsiders'**
A non-native speaker is someone whose mother tongue is different from the language that is used in the country she is staying or living in. An 'outsider' is anyone who is not from the main group such as an employee from another company, a member of a different family or someone who belongs to a different religion from the majority present. The 'outsider' is only an outsider while he is a minority: the label is transitory.

*Telling jokes:* it is insensitive and offensive to tell racist jokes, particularly in the hearing of someone from the race that is at the receiving end of the joke (see *Racism* in Chapter 18, page 192) or in front of anyone from a minority race – seeing that you are racist towards other people she will assume you are also racist towards her.

You can also offend unintentionally by being sarcastic: if the person at whom the joke is aimed is of a different culture there is a risk he will take your words literally, not understanding that you actually mean the opposite.

Suppose a representative from another country wants to buy chocolate from a vending machine but has only the notes given to him by the *bureau de change*. You offer to give him the coin he needs and waive his repeated offers of repayment. Saying as you hand it over, 'Don't spend it all at once' because of his vehemence over repaying you when the amount is worth so little to you can utterly bewilder him: first you offer him the money and refuse repayment but then behave as though it was a large amount that should be spent with care. He doesn't understand what you mean. Are you implying he spends a little too freely? Were you annoyed he hadn't insisted on repaying you? Did you not understand what the money was needed for? (The things in the vending machine *cost* the full value of the coin.)

*'In' jokes* that are particular to a company or institution have no meaning for outsiders. It is rude not to take their ignorance of your pet ways into consideration when you communicate with them. Similarly, don't use abbreviations for 'in' words with people from the outside. Saying, 'I'll meet you at the entrance of DH in half an hour' does not serve the purpose of arranging a meeting place when the other person hasn't a clue about what you mean.

*Colloquial English* may also prove difficult for a non-native speaker to understand; for example, saying, 'Let your hair down' instead of telling someone to relax and enjoy himself. You also need to be aware of differences between American English and UK English (see *Culture and spoken language* in Chapter 20, page 206).

Although it is common for groups of friends, or partners, to swear when together, it is not appropriate to swear when dealing with strangers, especially in a work environment. The other person will have every right to suspend further dealing with you and you will have lost credibility and the other person's respect. If you feel that you cannot get your point across without the use of swearing, you must not say your piece until you have calmed down and worked out a reasoned response that deals with the facts of the issue. You can say that you feel hurt or offended or angry but don't express these sentiments through swearing (see *Anger* in Chapter 13). It is also taboo to swear in public places, as many people will be affronted by your use of language, and many will be intimidated. If swearing is a habit, find alternative words that are acceptable to use and practise using them so that you reduce the chance of blurting out an offensive word when it matters.

*Euphemisms* are words that have usually been substituted for less palatable ones but you can sometimes annoy someone if you use them as it shows reluctance to be clear and to the point. Using euphemisms may also be interpreted as disapproval or an inability to talk freely, without embarrassment, on that particular subject. This puts a barrier between you and the other person. If you were a doctor or teacher giving a talk on sex education, you would confuse your young audience by discussing the male 'member' or patronising them with the use of 'willie'.

Talking about 'buns in the oven' or 'being in the club' may not necessarily be understood by another person as discussing a pregnancy, particularly for non-native speakers; nor might, 'kicking the bucket' (dying) or 'not washing your dirty linen in public' – instead say, 'It's not a good idea to argue in public and let everyone know your problems. You might regret it later and embarrass your family.'

In social situations it is often inappropriate to talk frankly about bodily functions, particularly at a formal function where people are eating. Here, if the subject must come up, it is considered more polite to use terminology such as 'relieving myself', 'going to powder my nose' (for women) or 'going to see a man about a dog' (for men), or just saying, 'Please excuse me' rather than stating your need to pee. North Americans like to say they need to visit the 'rest room' or 'wash room'.

### Feedback

Giving feedback lets someone know how she is doing, how well you understand what she's said, how she feels, and whether you agree with her: it is an essential part of good communication. When you receive feedback you will also know how you are doing – such as whether the other person likes you or approves of something you've done.

When giving feedback you might say, 'So what you think is . . . Well, it's not a bad idea but have you thought about . . .?' First you checked your understanding of the other person's viewpoint and then gave your opinion, after which you made a suggestion of a possible alternative. Or you might say, 'I'm not sure that I agree with you because . . .' Here you are not rejecting the idea without giving it some consideration; you are just explaining your doubts in a gentle way.

*Positive feedback* includes giving compliments (see Chapter 9), showing interest in the other person and what he has to say, and showing approval: for example, saying, 'You did absolutely the right thing. I'd have done exactly the same in your position.' This confirms the other person's action, making him feel good. All of these things help build rapport.

Positive feedback also includes smiling, looking at the other person encouragingly, hanging on to every word she says, making all the right noises at the right time, nodding approvingly, and joining in ('Oh, yes, that happened to me once when I . . .'). This is very rewarding, boosting her self-esteem, and makes her want to carry on talking to you. It also encourages her to strike up a second meeting, fostering liking and respect for you.

*Negative feedback* includes making complaints (see Chapter 12), giving criticism (see Chapter 15) and showing

dislike, a lack of interest in, and disapproval of, the other
person and what he has to say. Saying, 'I don't like how
you . . .' is a gentler way of saying, 'I think that's a stupid
idea' which is blunt and aggressive. When you give verbal
negative feedback, try to do it tactfully (see below) and
never criticise the person, only his behaviour or work.

Giving negative feedback also includes yawning, making the wrong noises at the wrong time or giving the wrong
responses, appearing to lose concentration and losing the
gist of what the other person is saying. These things are
very unrewarding and, if you get these signals, try a
different tack. Unfortunately, people with poor social
skills often fail to recognise the signals and may not even
realise they are boring or offensive, for example, and so
won't modify their behaviour for the next encounter.

*Vague feedback* involves doubt as to what the message
should be, so you need to ask for clarification. For example, if someone accuses you of ignoring her and you don't
think you have, ask her why she thinks that so any
misunderstanding can be cleared up:

*Person:*   Why do you ignore me when you see me in
            town?
*You:*      What do you mean?
*Person:*   On Saturday, when you came out of the build-
            ing society, I crossed the road right ahead of
            you. I smiled at you but you ignored me.
*You:*      I didn't ignore you, Charlotte, because I didn't
            see you.
*Person:*   You must have done, you were looking right at
            me.
*You:*      I may have been but I can't see far without my
            glasses. If I don't know what clothes you're
            wearing I can't identify you: faces are a com-
            plete blur. Why don't you wave next time or call
            out my name?

Any perceived damage that was done has been explained

and repaired and you have reached a better understanding of each other.

Vague feedback is unhelpful: if you don't understand what someone is trying to tell you, there is no value in what he says so you need to ask for clarification to understand how you're doing. For example, if someone says 'You always know what to say' ask, 'What do you mean?' or if someone says, 'You're always complaining about something' ask, 'What have I complained about?'

Whenever you give feedback, make sure it is specific. Here are some examples of vague unhelpful feedback followed by examples of specific helpful feedback (shown in italics).

'You make me sick.'
*'Seeing you pick your nose makes me feel ill.'*
'You never eat properly.'
*'Junk food is bad for you.'*
'It's a shame you're so unreliable.'
*'Twice when I've asked you to meet me to discuss your progress you failed to turn up.'*
'I never did like you.'
*'I find the jokes you make very distasteful.'*
'You're wonderful.'
*'It was very kind of you to stick up for me in front of the boss!'*

Listen carefully to the comments people make about others, especially when gossiping. If you hear someone say, 'Trust Mark to do that!' ask her what she means. Bad feelings about Mark can easily pass to other people without having any evidence to support the woman's comment, which is extremely unfair when Mark isn't present to stick up for himself. Be careful that you don't fall into similar difficulty. Only say things you can back up, or you'll look foolish if someone asks you for clarification.

*Giving clarification* is necessary when the other person misunderstands what you have said. For example, if someone replies to what you said by saying, 'I'm sorry to hear that you aren't coping with life at the moment' and this is not what you meant, you need to say, 'I think you misunderstood me. I do have lots of problems and it's hard going. But I *am* coping.'

### Tact

Being tactful avoids causing embarrassment and emotional pain; it is a higher-level social skill requiring an understanding of subtleties with which many people struggle. It is not lying, although an excess of tact can become lying as you give the person it is aimed at the wrong impression. A lack of tact results in bluntness, which can be very hurtful – so you need to try to achieve a middle ground between a complete lie and the absolute truth as you see it.

Suppose your friend has taken you shopping because she wants to buy a dress for a very important party and wants your help and advice, but the dress she falls in love with looks dreadful on her. An extreme cover up response would be to say, 'The dress really suits you.' But this would be unkind as that's probably just what she wants to hear and, relying on your opinion, she will buy the dress and look ridiculous. In the long run she will get the message that it doesn't do anything for her and she will not thank you for your over kind words.

A blunt response would be to say, 'You look like the back end of a bus.' This level of candour will hurt your friend's feelings and she will feel bad about herself. A tactful response would be to choose a middle ground by saying that the colour doesn't suit her or that it doesn't flatter her bust line or that the first dress she tried on did a lot more for her. You could say that the colour wasn't suitable for the venue and that a subdued tone would be more appropriate, if that's true. Or you could say, 'I'm not sure why I feel reserved about the dress – but there's something not quite right. I think we should keep looking.' Remember that your friend cannot help how she looks so needs a sensitive approach that stops her from making the wrong decision – and making a fool of herself in public.

If she insists on buying the dress despite your gentle efforts, you must allow her the responsibility to make her own decision. She had asked for your opinion and you gave it. It is then up to her whether or not she follows your advice. Don't crush her by telling her she looks silly in it: she may reconsider when she tries it on at home, deciding you are right after all. People go on hearing what has been said to them long after the words have been spoken and your words may not be forgotten. But, if she does not change her mind, you must accept that she does have the right to make her own mistakes. And who are you to judge? If she likes the dress that much and feels good and confident wearing it, that's fine: she hopefully won't know any different.

When you are invited to eat a meal someone else has prepared, it is polite to be complimentary about it whatever your private opinion. Laci was served corn on the cob as a starter and when the host asked him if he liked it he replied, 'Where I come from we grow this to feed the pigs.' His tone implied he didn't consider corn was suitable for human consumption. In a nutshell, Laci told his host he had just served him pig food, which, as well as insulting the host, put a damper on the rest of the meal. Try to think before you say something and ask yourself if it is likely to offend or hurt the other person's feelings.

*Use of silence in tact*. Sometimes it is best to keep quiet and not say anything at all. For example, if someone gives you a tie or a scarf for a gift and he says, 'I know your favourite colour is yellow so I thought you'd like this', you should not immediately reply with, 'Actually, my favourite colour's blue.' The best thing to do is to ignore the comment about your favourite colour and thank him for his kindness.

Ruth kept sneezing at a friend's house and he asked her if she had a cold, to which she replied no. Then he suggested that she might have an allergy and that perhaps he'd put on too much aftershave. She denied the suggestion of aftershave and kept quiet about the real culprit: dust. To proffer this as an explanation would imply that her friend's home was dirty and it might offend.

If you go into a toilet after someone else has come out, it is embarrassing to the other person to comment on any smell that might be lingering or show by wrinkling your nose that anything is amiss. And, when you return to the group you were with, it should not be mentioned, even if the other person is not part of that group.

*Use of eyes and speech in tact.* Just as it is sometimes tactful to remain silent on a certain point, it is sometimes tactful to pretend you have not seen something or find it of such little interest that you easily avert your eyes to save the other person embarrassment. For example, if someone has just spilt his dinner down himself at a formal function and does not need assistance clearing the mess, try to avert your eyes so that you do not make him feel more self-conscious or embarrassed: and never laugh unless the person laughs first and is in your group of friends and you all laugh together.

If someone comes out of the toilet and his trouser zip is undone, or a woman comes out with her skirt tucked up in her knickers, you should quietly point it out to the person and then avert your gaze while he or she makes the necessary adjustments. Don't smile unless the other person does first.

*Use of laughter in tact.* Sometimes you need to pretend that it is the first time ever that you have heard a particular joke so as not to offend the person telling it or not to spoil it for others. Suppose you work for a campsite holiday company called Sunsites and a customer says to you after his first week of rain, 'Sunsites? More like Rainysites.' You need to smile politely or give a small chuckle, or he will be offended and feel aggrieved with the company. He is not to know (although many could guess) that you had heard it many times before.

*Faux pas* is French for an embarrassing mistake. These are very common and can make you want to disappear and be swallowed up into the ground. But unfortunately, your words are likely to ring around the room as silence falls and everyone looks your way. Probably the most common *faux pas* to make is that of a lack of tact or a lack of thought in colloquial English. Some examples of these are:

*'Don't say that or he'll have a fit.'*

This is a common British expression. But is not taken kindly by those suffering from epilepsy.

*'Are you deaf or something?'*

Too late, you see the hearing aid.

*'Do you see (my point)?'*

You are explaining to a visually challenged person.

Other *faux pas* can be made by foreigners using English expressions. A man once said to a woman, 'It's probably happened more often than you've had clean underwear.' Mentioning a woman's underwear whether clean or dirty is a mistake, but implying that she has dirty underwear would embarrass her. The correct expression should have been, '. . . more often than you've had hot dinners.'

You don't even have to be a foreigner to get your idioms wrong. A British man said of a woman, 'Men are attracted to her like flies round a lump of sh..' When I spoke to him about it, he admitted that he thought it wasn't quite right. It should have been, 'Men are attracted to her like bees around a honey pot.'

Another pitfall is speaking out before you have all the facts. My husband and I were invited to my friend's new flat to see the work that had been done on it. Much of the flat had been gutted and was being brought into shape room by room. It was still only half complete when we went to see it. Without waiting to check the state of the living room from my friend's perspective, my husband said, 'It will look nice when it's decorated.' Unfortunately that was one of the finished rooms. Oops.

If you have made a *faux pas*, take your cue from the person you feel you offended. If she and the people around you carry on regardless, you can let your slip go. Drawing attention to it by making a big show of apology might make things worse instead of better. However, with major blunders – such as my husband's – admit your error straight away and apologise to clear the air.

If another person seemingly ignores your *faux pas* she has hopefully seen it as you intended – an innocent remark made because of the frequency of its use in the English language. If it is an insensitive remark because of a frequently used translated expression from your culture that differs from hers, explain this to her. If you have obviously offended the other person say, 'I'm sorry, that was a tactless expression. It's one I've used so many times that I blurted it out without thinking. I did not mean to hurt your feelings or appear insensitive.'

# 12

# DEALING WITH CONFLICT: LEARNING TO NEGOTIATE

Two people, or parties, are in conflict when they each want something different and have opposing views. If neither side is prepared to budge, neither side can 'win', and you have complete conflict. This aggressive, unyielding stance can build resentment between people. It is also unproductive as you have an impasse and nothing can change. Complete capitulation is a passive response where you 'lose' and the other person 'wins'. The other person will feel pleased with herself and you will feel bad about yourself. Agreeing to some sort of compromise is an assertive response and both sides have a measure of winning and can be satisfied with the outcome.

### Compromise and negotiation

A compromise is a mutually acceptable arrangement that benefits both sides although it is not completely what either side wants. But by compromising, both sides can be considered to 'win': they each have something that they want out of the situation. Suppose you have a long way to travel to work each day and you have a demanding job. To cope with the working week you have decided not to go out in the evenings but to socialise only on weekends, but your friend has invited the people in your department out for drinks and a meal after work to celebrate his birthday. You don't want to feel left out or have your friend feel rejected by you, but neither do you want to be very late home. The others all live much closer to work. You could say, 'I'd love to join you for a drink, but I'll give the meal a miss. I'd get home too late.'

If the conflict is major and complex, and it is likely that emotions are going to get involved, try to keep things cool. Work out between you the things on which you can both agree. Then work out your priorities and decide on which things you are prepared to compromise and on which things you want to stand firm, while the other person does the same. Then discuss them to see if you can come up with a workable solution: don't haggle over things low down on your list of priorities.

For example, you want to job share with a friend while you both study part-time and, although it is working mainly evenings and weekends, there are some areas of difficulty:

● Neither of you wants to work Friday and Saturday evenings because of wanting to socialise on those evenings.

● Both of you want to work Sundays as there's double pay on Sundays.

● You have mutual friends so you both want to attend the same birthday parties and other celebrations.

● You don't want to find a different job, as it would be hard to get one with hours that suit.

● You sometimes need to stay at college late and you like the flexibility of being able to swap shifts with your friend. With fixed hours you wouldn't be able to do this.

Conversation to negotiate what to do could go like this:

*You:*      Both of us want the same things but obviously we can't have them. Let's try and work out how

|  |  |
|---|---|
| | we can both get *some* of the things we want. |
| *Friend:* | OK. |
| *You:* | Shall we make a rota so that if you work on a Friday evening you have Saturday evening off and then the following week, I'd work Friday evening and have Saturday evening off? That way we'd both have an evening out on the weekend every week. |
| *Friend:* | What if we need two Fridays off in a row? |
| *You:* | We could do a monthly rota where it works out that we've shared out the Fridays and Saturdays. And we could work every other Sunday to make sure the extra pay is shared fairly too. |
| *Friend:* | That's fine. But what about when we both want to go to a party because it's one of our friends' birthdays? |
| *You:* | Perhaps we could ask the manager if she could arrange for someone else to cover for us – and if she can't, we could take it in turns. But she probably could as she has to have people to cover when someone's off sick. |

With the above arrangement, you and the other person 'win' an equal amount of the time. If you couldn't agree on the working arrangement both of you would 'lose'. If you were passive and gave in to your friend's demands, you would 'lose' and feel very aggrieved while your friend would 'win' and be happy to have the ideal job even though he wasn't playing fair.

Suppose your boss wants holiday plans submitted by March so that cover can be organised well in advance and there is a rule that only one key member of each department can go away at any one time. You are new to the company so you get last choice of the available holiday dates and they do not suit your plans. You could say, 'I have a difficulty with the summer holiday arrangements. My partner works at *Drayman's* and can't have the two weeks off in July that you have allocated to me. I understand that I haven't been here long enough to qualify for annual leave yet but would it be possible to make an exception and let me take my two weeks in April so that I can go away with my partner? Then I would be available for all of July and August to help cover the other absences.'

Here you have shown that you have thought about how the change would benefit the company as well as yourself – although you don't end up with a summer holiday – so your boss would see that there is good reasoning behind your suggestion, making it harder for her to refuse.

Sometimes it is hard coming to a compromise because there are so many people involved. For example, you are getting married but you, your partner, your parents and his parents all want different things. You cannot agree on a convenient time, a suitable venue for the reception or the type of food that will be served. You talk to your partner alone about it. You could say, 'There are too many people having a say in our wedding. Why don't the two of us sort out what we want first, while being aware of our parents' opinions, and come to some sort of compromise? It is our day so ultimately the wedding should be decided by us.'

If necessary, put the difficulties before someone else to see if she can spot a solution you have not been able to, being too close to the problem.

### Making deals: reward/penalty system

Often, negotiation is about making deals with people: 'If I do this, will you do that?' When making deals, or showing someone where your boundaries lie, it is useful to use a *reward* and *penalty* system which involves telling the other person how you will behave towards her or what you will do if she doesn't comply with your (reasonable) wishes. This has nothing to do with giving intimidating threats, which is aggressive behaviour.

Suppose your digital camera is faulty so you take it back to the shop where you bought it and ask for a new one. The shop assistant tells you to send it to the repair centre. You are not satisfied with this as you have had the camera for less than a month and believe it was not of 'merchantable quality' when you bought it as it broke down so soon.

*Reward:*   I'd appreciate having my digital camera replaced as it's faulty and less than a month old.

*Penalty:*   If you can't do that, I'd like to see the manager.

Your partner keeps borrowing your shirts and jumpers and then returns them in a dirty condition. You then don't have clean clothes for work when you need them.

*Reward:*   I don't mind you borrowing my clothes as long as you look after them and wash and iron them after you've worn them.

*Penalty:*   If you can't do that then don't borrow my clothes again.

You can also use the reward/penalty system to show someone that you stand firm on a particular point and will do something, either positive or negative – this does not include aggressive threats – depending on how she alters her behaviour. For example, a friend of yours flirts with any man, whether or not 'available', including your partner.

*Reward:*   Randa, I don't mind when you flirt with other men.
           But I do mind when it's my partner. I noticed you sat rather close to Imran and you kept touching his arm. I don't appreciate your familiarity with him and it makes me feel very uncomfortable.

*Penalty:*   If you don't stop doing it we can't continue being friends.

Suppose a colleague at work knew that you'd gone to another department to pick up some files but, when your boss asked him where you were, he said he thought you'd gone to the loo, implying you waste much time by frequent unnecessary visits to the toilet.

*Reward:*  When you need to go on an errand I always explain your absence if necessary. I'm happy to continue doing that.

*Penalty:*  But if you ever imply I've bunked off again, I'll be sure to lose my memory too.

### Conflict and complaints

When people have a complaint to make they are in conflict with the person or company they feel has injured them in some way (also see Chapter 15). Often they will not listen to any kind of reasoning until their anger has been diffused (see *Anger* in Chapter 13, page 145). Once an angry person has calmed down, you can try to understand what the problem is and mutually work at sorting it out until you are both satisfied with the outcome, even though it might not be quite as either of you expected or hoped.

Imagine you are working for customer service in a large department store. Someone has just demanded his money back on an item of clothing for which he has no receipt. If you immediately say, 'I can't do that' you will create conflict as negative statements annoy people and make them deaf to what you have to say. Instead say, 'The store policy is only to give refunds with proofs of purchase. If you'd got the receipt I'd have gladly done as you'd asked. Have you considered exchanging it for something else? Or would you prefer to have a voucher so you can choose something another time?' Consulting the customer shows that you are treating her with respect and that you are trying to be helpful within the boundaries set by your employer. Giving the customer a choice may also help diffuse a potentially conflicting situation by giving her time to think, lessening the chance of her giving a disappointed knee-jerk reaction.

*Compromise and complaints.* You may be restricted in

what you can offer an angry customer by your employer, but if you are the manager, there is no reason why you should not try your best to meet the customer half way.

When my daughter was five, I bought her a pair of trainers with a Velcro fastening. Before she had outgrown them the Velcro lost its tackiness and did not hold the shoe on. The manager of the shoe shop refused to exchange them and refused to accept that the trainer should outlast the child's growth, despite the shoe having cost a great deal of money. I wrote to Head Office and was told that the shoe should indeed outlast the child's growth and that the manager should have offered to pay for their repair; Head Office refunded the cost of the repair to me. I achieved my goal of having a pair of trainers that my daughter could wear until she outgrew them at no further expense; the company also 'won' because the cost to it was minimal. Had the shop manager suggested a repair as a compromise, I would not have complained to Head Office about her and she would have kept me as a customer for future purchases.

*Conflict in the workplace* can be prevented through communication, which is a vital aspect of working with other people. However, for this to create harmony both bosses and subordinates need to play the game.

If you have people working under you, consider how you treat them: do you give regular opportunities for feedback on how either you or they are doing, or on matters relating to company policy? And, if you do give them the opportunity to speak, do you respect them by listening and taking notice of their comments?

How well do you know your colleagues? If, for example, someone is having problems outside the work environment are you able to take those into account when you deal with him? If not, you could be seen to be unfeeling. If you are approachable and behave in ways to command respect then staff should feel confident about confiding in you.

When you give feedback to colleagues is it always negative or do you remember to praise as well? And, when you do need to criticise, is it constructive? This means not saying, 'That's wrong. Do it again' but, 'If you do it like this, you get a better finish.' And do you suggest ways your staff as a group and as individuals can improve? If you criticise every small thing that a member of your staff does wrong you will create conflict: try to correct important mistakes while allowing some freedom to make small errors without consequences. Once the bigger mistakes have been dealt with, you can gradually address others. When you see a mistake made, do you stay calm in your dealings with your staff or do you lose your temper? If you are frequently angry and unpredictable, you will be seen as unapproachable and your staff members will keep their distance.

If you work as a subordinate, consider how you relate to those in a superior position to you. When you need to say something important to your boss do you pick your time carefully or go right ahead regardless of what's going on around you? You are unlikely to have your requests met if you irritate your boss by not taking into account that she is working to avert a crisis or already has someone with her. And tackling her in a corridor when on the way to a meeting is not conducive to a lengthy and private chat where both of you can give your full attention to the matter you want to discuss. When you think you've judged the right time, do you check this with your boss by asking if it's convenient?

If you expect understanding from your boss when you are under par, do you allow she has the right to expect you to understand back when she's not feeling her best? If you have hopes of being promoted in the company structure, are you ready to volunteer to take on extra tasks? Do you ask for advice on how to improve? Do you watch your superiors to see how they do things and try to model them with appropriate adaptations for your individual character? Or do you expect it is your right to be promoted just on the strength of the number of years you have been working there without regard to your performance and motivation?

# 13

# EXPRESSING FEELINGS

Intimacy calls for the exchange of feelings about situations that have happened or feelings about other people. This enables people to gain a greater understanding of one another and gives them the opportunity to empathise. Unfortunately, many people find it hard to show their feelings or explain how they feel but not showing feelings can act as a barrier, preventing friendships from becoming close.

It is essential in long-term sexual relationships to be able to communicate openly and honestly about the way you feel about things that have happened and the way you feel about each other. For example, if you really love someone, it's a bit dampening not to let her know. You may think that showing her is sufficient but it does not have nearly the same impact as saying, 'I love you.'

### Expressing feelings to help conversation flow

For any social interaction, without exchanging viewpoints on subjects, the conversation can seem flat and stilted, rather like an exchange of statements. Saying something about the way you feel about everyday things to help conversation flow is low-risk disclosure (looked at in Chapter 2) that helps others get to know you and encourages them to disclose similarly.

Imagine someone at work asks you how your weekend went. If you reply, 'Fine', there is little response that he could give to this. If you were talking to someone you knew well, or saw regularly, it would have made sense to say more, to improve the understanding between you and help the relationship develop: you do need to be able to get on well with those you work with and show that you enjoy talking to others or you will be ostracised and considered standoffish. So you could have said, 'Actually, it wasn't great. My brother-in-law descended on us without warning so we had to cancel the meal out we'd planned. Although it was nice to see him he often just turns up and assumes we're free.' Here you have shown part of your life to the other person and when you ask how his weekend was, he will be encouraged by your response to give more than a one-word answer.

Imagine your granddaughter is the first member of your entire family to have got into university and you want to share the news with friends. Now is a time to express just how you feel so that others know what it means to you and so will know how to respond. You could say, 'I'm so happy I just had to spread the news. Vicky's done it! She's got to university. I'm so proud of her. The first in our family to have done it. I haven't felt this ecstatic in years.'

If you know there is something lacking in your relationships, try to be more open with your feelings.

### Personality and feelings

*Aggressive people* are often too afraid to show the gentler side of their nature so try to hide their softer emotions of love, tenderness, sadness and grief for fear of being laughed at or considered weak. But in never showing vulnerability, you do not get people to warm towards you and you end up pushing them away, preventing the development of intimate relationships. And, because you have not divulged how you feel about things no one will understand you, which can make you feel very lonely.

*Passive people* are not used to describing their feelings as they feel no one will want to listen or that others will think them stupid for feeling that way. Many passive people are women – due to cultural, religious and traditional upbringings. However, most women seem to express their feelings better than most men. Women tend to be much more likely to get emotional support from one another, as they tend to disclose their feelings more frequently and value sharing them.

*Assertive people* are comfortable in the knowledge that they are important to their friends and that their friends would want to know when they are in trouble so that they can give help and support. They are not afraid to divulge how they feel to trusted friends or to seek help from a professional when it is more appropriate.

### Emotional feelings list

Many people find it easier to talk about physical feelings, such as feeling hot, cold or sore, than emotional feelings. Their vulnerabilities, they feel, are best left hidden; or they are just too ill at ease to reveal them. But if they become used to telling people how they feel, they will be more comfortable with hearing about other people's feelings and will more easily be able to lend a sympathetic ear and have intimate, caring relationships.

As so many people have trouble expressing emotional feelings, a list is provided below. Try to widen your usage of feelings expressions and see what a difference it makes to your relationships.

- Abandoned
- Accepted
- Adventurous
- Affectionate
- Alone

- Ambitious
- Angry
- Anxious
- Appreciated
- Bereft
- Bitter
- Bored
- Calm
- Cheated
- Cheerful
- Competitive
- Concerned
- Confident
- Confused
- Contented
- Cool
- Daring
- Decisive
- Dependent
- Depressed
- Desperate
- Disappointed
- Disbelieving
- Disgusted
- Distraught
- Eager
- Embarrassed
- Empty inside
- Envious
- Exasperated
- Excited
- Flustered
- Frantic
- Frightened
- Frustrated
- Furious

- Glad
- Guilty
- Happy
- Hard hearted
- Homesick
- Hopeful
- Humiliated
- Hurt
- Impatient
- In control
- In love
- Inferior
- Insecure
- Interested
- Intimidated
- Irritated
- Jealous
- Joyful
- Let down
- Lonely
- Mad
- Numb
- Optimistic
- Overwhelmed
- Pessimistic
- Powerless
- Protective
- Relaxed
- Resentful
- Responsible
- Sad
- Satisfied
- Scared
- Shy
- Sorrowful
- Strange

- Supported
- Suspicious
- Sympathetic
- Taken advantage of
- Tearful
- Tense
- Thrilled
- Unappreciated
- Unattractive
- Uncomfortable
- Understanding
- Unhappy
- Unloved
- Unwanted
- Upset
- Uptight
- Used
- Vulnerable
- Weird
- Wonderful
- Worried
- Wronged

### Anger

If you repress angry feelings so that they build up inside you, they can become destructive. It is better to let them out in a positive and controlled way as they occur; or they can leave you tense and irritable, interfere with your concentration, give you bad dreams and symptoms of anxiety, and can even lead to a breakdown. Bottled up feelings can also make you behave in an inappropriate way, having an exaggerated response to a small event, getting it out of proportion: you might also unfairly take out your problems on someone close to you.

*Aggressive people* often show their anger too readily and in an uncontrolled way by yelling, throwing things and physically hurting others. Being a bully only shows you can shout louder than other people and hit harder. It does not get you any bonus points for communication skills. Nor does it show you as being intelligent and in control of your own feelings and bodily actions. You'd be far more admired for a skilful handling of a situation, deliberately controlling your behaviour because you have judged the situation inappropriate for a display of out-of-control anger.

*Passive people* are often too afraid to show anger or annoyance for fear of upsetting people and having to deal with the consequences or because they cannot face giving free rein to their emotions. They are more likely to suffer in silence or moan to a friend behind the person's back. Not showing anger when it is appropriate means that the person who is at fault will get away with unacceptable behaviour and may repeat that behaviour with other people.

*Assertive people* can choose whether they wish to show their anger. There may be very good reasons why hiding their anger would be appropriate. For example, if someone has just suffered bereavement it would be silly to worry him about an extra dent he's just made in the family car. When assertive people do show anger, they never physically hurt someone and they can adjust their level of anger to fit the circumstance and the person at whom it is directed.

**Inappropriate anger**
People do not respond well if you are clumsy in the way you show feelings, such as shouting at someone when she doesn't deserve it, or by walking out of the room when she is talking to you in a reasonable way: this is only appropriate when you are being verbally or physically abused; otherwise stand your ground and say what you feel.

Shouting at your partner, because he forgot to make you

a cup of tea with his, makes it unlikely he'll offer to bring you a drink again. Instead say: 'Never mind, I'll get my own.' It's not such a big deal; you can let this one slide. However, if the tea-making issue is long-standing rather than a one-off event, then it would be appropriate to get angry: 'I've told you several times that it's rude and inconsiderate to make yourself a drink and forget about me. Why don't you take any notice?'

Anger is also inappropriate if you want to complain about something while wanting something in return such as a change in someone's behaviour or for a shop assistant to exchange a faulty item: she would not be in the right frame of mind to cooperate with you or listen to your needs if you'd shouted at her.

**Appropriate anger**
If the situation is rather more vital than someone once forgetting to bring you a cup of tea, you have a right to get angry and explain exactly how you feel, otherwise the person is likely to do the same again because he does not understand the effect of his actions.

Imagine you've been waiting all day for an important telephone call from another company, but have to go out for a short while. You expect the call to be dealt with properly by your secretary in your absence. However, he fails to take a message, fails to inform the caller that you'll be back in five minutes and does not think to take down the caller's number so that you can return the call. You could say, 'You knew I was waiting for that call! I'd told you how important it was and you didn't even get his number so I could call him back! That was incompetent of you!'

Imagine you have just found out that your best friend has recently slept with your long-standing partner. You could say, 'I feel betrayed. Your sleeping with Simon has devastated me. I feel nothing but contempt for what you have done and contempt for the two-faced behaviour you have shown towards me. I never want to see or hear from you again.'

## Dealing with your own anger

When you are enraged and hurting, the immediate instinct is to fight back: if you were hurt physically, you might want to hurt the other person physically back; if something hurtful was said, you may want to say something equally or more hurtful back. To deal with your anger in an appropriate way:

- Don't do anything immediately.
- Try to keep calm and organise your thoughts logically. Acting when in a rage is unwise as you might be embarrassed afterwards or do damage, whether physical or emotional, that you will later regret. Hasty words can never be unsaid.
- Check the facts. Have you evidence of what has happened? If not, find it.
- Ask yourself why the other person may have done this. Is there a perspective that you have not considered?
- What has happened in the past? Perhaps what has recently happened stems from some past grudge or grievance.
- If you know that you won't be able to talk to the other person in a calm and rational way, leave the situation and give yourself time to reflect. You won't achieve anything by being enraged and illogical.
- When you are ready to talk, tell the other person how you feel about what was done or said and how you feel about him. Also say what you want – such as an apology or a promise to make amends in some way. If the person is not prepared to do that, have a penalty ready such as not wanting to go out with the person any more or not being prepared to do him another favour.

**Diffusing another person's anger**

A good way to diffuse someone else's anger (also see *Conflict and complaints* in Chapter 12, page 136) is wholly to agree on something that is genuinely true. Then, when the person has calmed down because she feels you have listened to what she has said, she will be more interested in what you have to say. Use this opportunity to explain what you do disagree with and why. Only accept the part of the blame that is yours; reject the rest and explain why the other person is mistaken. Keep calm so that you don't fuel her emotion. Show that you are in command of the situation, even if you don't feel you are. And don't impress your superiority or authority over her, as that would fire an already frustrated person into more anger rather than diffusing it.

Suppose you work as a waiter and a couple prepare to leave the restaurant without finishing the meal and without offering to pay.

*You:*        Excuse me, Sir, Madam. Is there something wrong?

*Customer:*   You're damn right there's something wrong. You have treated us abominably in this restaurant and we're leaving. My food was cold and had already congealed when it arrived and my wife's order was wrong. It's disgraceful calling yourself a restaurant with such crap service. You told me the order would take only twenty minutes but we had to wait three quarters of an hour for food that was bloody inedible!

*You:*        I'm very sorry that you are disappointed with the service here. I understand that you are upset about the meal. Please sit down and let me help sort things out.

*Customer:*   Well?

*You:*        You're right, I did tell you that there was a twenty-minute wait and I'm sorry that I had

misjudged the timing. If you wouldn't mind
waiting, I'll get the manager for you so that
she can record your complaint while I speak
to the chef. We do take pride in our work and
take all complaints seriously. I can assure you
we rarely have a dissatisfied customer. What
has happened today has been very unfortunate and we will do all we can to put matters
right.

Offering to help and lending a sympathetic ear – while not
necessarily accepting all the blame but behaving as an
impartial observer – helps to diffuse the customer's anger.
The manager will have to suggest a solution to satisfy the
customer and stop open conflict in front of other diners.

Sometimes, you need to make repeated requests such as
when dealing with an angry customer over the telephone:
'I am sorry, but as I said, I can't deal with your complaint
until I have entered your reference number which gives me
access to your records.' Then you can invite him to tell you
in a calm and coherent fashion what the problem is:
'Please sir, try to keep calm. I can understand you are
upset and I want to help sort this out. Now that I have
your details on screen I can enter the information you give
me so that I can pass you on to the best person to deal
with this. When did you say this event occurred?'

# 14

# ASKING FOR WHAT YOU WANT

Aggressive people can be very successful at getting their own way although they do not necessarily achieve this through positive behaviour, caring for no one's needs excepting their own. Passive people are unlikely to get what they want either because they don't ask for it in the first place or because they ask in such a way that makes it easy for others to refuse; they show they don't really expect a positive response. If you are to succeed at getting people to listen to your needs or to reconsider a previous decision *and* keep their respect, you need to ask assertively so that you relate to them on an equal footing without causing animosity and resentment, or allowing them to take advantage of a gentle nature.

### Aggressive ways of getting what you want
*You can aggressively get people to do things for you* by emotional blackmail: 'Your mum would be really disappointed if she knew you refused to help a friend in need' or, 'I'm sure such a kind person as you wouldn't refuse an old friend . . .' and by manipulation: pretending to like someone so that he'll do something for you, and by threats: 'If you don't do this for me, I'll tell your Dad you . . .' or, 'If you don't do it, I'll tell everyone you slept with me.'

It is also possible to persuade someone to do something you want by telling a lie: by promising to do one thing if she does the other and then not carrying through your part of the bargain. Suppose you are a mature student sharing a house with someone on a different course from you and your exams are before the other person's. You come to an arrangement that would, on the surface, benefit you both, but in the end only benefits you. You suggest, 'If you cook all our meals and do all the washing while I'm studying for my exams, I'll do the same for you when mine are over to give you a free rein at studying.' So, she does all the work while you study. But when her exams loom, you push off home or on holiday.

*You can aggressively do things for others* by assuming you know what they need and taking it upon yourself to sort it out, thinking that you're doing them a favour. For example, deciding that someone's house is dirty or that his garden is badly overgrown and personally putting it to rights, or organising someone else to do it, without his consent; or redecorating your mum's bedroom, without her knowledge or consent, for when she gets out of hospital after a long stay.

Giving something as a gift that another person feels unable to accept – because of its high value or inappropriateness – and insisting that she keeps it is also an aggressive act. So is sending off a memo to others, without consultation, when you are encroaching on an area for which another person is responsible; or buying an expensive birthday present for your dad when you expect your siblings to contribute and you haven't consulted whether they want to give a combined present or indeed whether they approve of your choice and its cost.

Aggressive people tend to get embarrassed about offering help. They prefer to get stuck in, doing the thing their way and at their own convenience, rather than respecting the other person's right to refuse.

**Passive ways of asking for what you want**

Asking for what you want in a passive way is not likely to get you what you want. It shows the other person that you are expecting her to say no. These approaches are unlikely to get a positive response:

- 'Would you mind terribly if . . .?'
- 'I was wondering, if it wasn't too much trouble . . .?'
- 'If you have time, and you're not too busy, could you fit in . . .?'
- 'I don't suppose . . .?'

**Assertive ways of asking for what you want**

A direct and honest approach when asking for what you want, using assertive body language to reinforce your words without showing that you're worried about being refused, is much more likely to get you the response you'd like. For example, if you want your colleague to buy you some coffee in her lunch break it would not be sensible to use either of these requests:

*Aggressive request:* I see you're off out. You can get me a jar of coffee while you're gone.

*Passive request:* Oh, are you going out? Have you got much to do? Are you in a hurry? I wonder, if you don't mind, and of course, I'll perfectly understand if you do, would it be possible, if you have time, to get me some coffee?

Being direct but respectful and explaining why you need your colleague to do you a favour is much more likely to get a positive response:

*Assertive request:* I've run out of coffee. If you're going out, I'd really appreciate it if you could get me a jar of X. I'm working right through today as this has got to be finished for 9 am tomorrow.

Other examples of asking assertively are: 'I'm going to be

late home tomorrow. Could you cook the evening meal?' and, 'Would you be offended if I changed the T-shirt? I don't think the colour suits me' and, 'Please don't buy the children quite so many sweets. They'll appreciate you just as much and have better teeth.'

### Asking for cooperation

Explaining your needs makes it more likely that other people will meet you half way. For example, you want to throw a party but live in close community with others: it would be polite to inform your neighbours of the forth-coming event as you don't want to be reported to the police for disturbing the peace – and you want their goodwill. The best way to do this is to invite your nearest neighbours to the party and, for those not invited, you could tell them how many people are expected and at what time the party will start and finish. Although you are not asking outright for permission – it would be silly to allow one neighbour to stop you having your party – you are asking to have a fun party: should someone have qualms over the likely noise she is given the opportunity to voice her opinion.

For the closest neighbours, you could say, 'Hello. I'm having a party on Saturday night and would like to invite you and your partner. There will be about 30 to 40 people, mainly friends from work, but I'm also inviting the neigh-bours on the other side of me. It starts at 9 pm (and I expect it to finish around 1 am). Do you think you'll be able to come?'

For the uninvited, you could say, 'Hello. I'm Diane Chan. I live at number 24 and want to let you know that I'm planning to have a party on Saturday night. I hope you won't be too disturbed by it. I've invited about 30 to 40 people to come around 9 pm. I expect most to have left by 12 and for the party to finish by 1 am. Here's my telephone number: if the music disturbs you too much, give me a call and I'll turn the volume down. It will definitely be turned down after midnight in any case. I have no wish to fall out with you over my party so if anything happens that you're not happy about, please let me know.'

Your neighbours would be even more understanding if there was a special reason for the party which you told them about such as: your son's bar-mitzvah or twenty-first; your fortieth; your daughter's engagement party; your flat-warming party; a party to celebrate your promotion or retirement or wedding anniversary. This introduces the human element and many would look more kindly on a noisy celebration than a party for the sake of it. But don't lie: they would feel cheated if they were to find out.

**Asking to be taken seriously**
It may be that someone doesn't listen to you properly or take what you say seriously enough. If this is the case, you need to try again in a way that will make her listen. Imagine you are concerned about your granddaughter's speech. Your daughter, Cerys, is very defensive about it and insists there is nothing wrong but you'd like a professional opinion: 'Cerys, I know I've brought this up before but I am concerned for Hattie. I only want what's best for her. I know you've said there is nothing wrong with the development of her speech but it does still worry me. Even if it's just to put a silly old woman's mind at rest, I'd really appreciate a professional opinion. Then I need never bring up the subject again.'

**Asking someone to do you a favour**
If you want something from someone else, you must ask in a straightforward way, treat him as an equal and be polite. Let him know why he's the most appropriate person to ask or explain why you can't do it yourself – unless it's obvious. Also, show gratitude in an appropriate amount, but don't be ingratiating.

Imagine you have just lost your day's work on the computer as a file was overwritten by mistake. You know that you can't leave until you've redone it, but you have to pick up your children from school. You call the parent of one of your children's friends to ask if he can collect them and give them tea. 'Hi Brian, it's Sinead. I'm ringing to ask a big favour. I've hit a problem at work – I lost the file I was working on and have to redo it before I can leave. Would you mind picking up the kids from school and feeding them? I should be through by seven, but please say if it's not convenient . . . You can? Thanks so much. You've saved my day. And they always have a great time at your place. I hope you'll call on me when you're stuck.'

## Asking someone to change his or her behaviour

If someone has done or said something to upset you, you might want to do something about it. If it's something that happens time and again, you really ought to say something.

- Concentrate on the person's behaviour: What happened? When did it happen? Has it happened before?
- Start your sentence with 'I' or any other word but *not* 'You'. Don't accuse.
- Be clear about what it is you don't like and state it.
- Be clear about what you want done and state it.
- Use the person's name, if possible.

Imagine your friend said she'd meet you in the pub at 8 pm. You were there on time but she was half an hour late. You felt very uncomfortable because a group of three men kept looking at you from the bar, making comments about you and laughing. Then one of them came over to your table while the other two watched encouragingly. The man tried to persuade you to leave with him. You had difficulty in getting him to understand no. When your friend arrives, you could say, 'I've just had a terrible time waiting for you. This is the third time you've been late,

Clarice. I'm not going to meet you in a pub again.'

If something has been happening to upset you on a regular basis, you should warn the other person to give her a chance to put things right, otherwise it can be interpreted as an aggressive response. However, if there is an overriding reason why you should not give the person another chance, explain how her behaviour has affected you. For example, you go on holiday with a friend who, the night you arrive, meets someone in the bar. From then on she spends all her time with him, leaving you on your own for the duration of the holiday. You could say, 'Lisa, I thought we were going away together, to keep each other company. But you dropped me the night we arrived and I had to go everywhere by myself. I'm not ever going away with you again. And unless you show me more consideration in the future we may as well stop being friends.'

## Asking to change your behaviour

If someone has been used to you doing something on a regular basis, it would be abrupt and aggressive suddenly to stop or change the way in which you did it without first offering an explanation or consulting the other person over it. Imagine you regularly go with someone collecting door-to-door or collecting in the street for a good cause but for medical reasons you have to stop. It would be inappropriate to let him down on the day of the collection. Instead, you could say either of these things: 'I know that you're collecting next month. I want to let you know that I shan't be able to help again because my arthritis has got so much worse. I wanted to tell you early so that you'd have a chance of finding someone else' or, 'I'm afraid this will have to be the last time I come collecting with you. My arthritis is so bad I just can't do it any more.'

If your behaviour vastly changes from the norm, it is a good idea to explain why to the people around you so that they can understand rather than unfairly criticise you for it: you are more likely to get sympathy and understanding rather than hassle and snide comments over what others would perceive as unreasonable behaviour. For example, you came home last night to find your home had been broken into. Although you generally have a sweet temperament, you are now feeling angry at the world. You explain why you are in such a bad mood: 'I'm very bristly today because my flat's been burgled and they've trashed the place. Please ignore my bad temper.'

### Asking for help

Many people find it hard to ask for help at all, let alone in a skilful way, because of insecurity, low self-esteem and a lack of confidence. They may not want to admit that they cannot cope, are vulnerable, are too stupid to understand, or are unable to repay the debt. Or they may feel that it is a sign of strength to be completely self-reliant but it's really a sign of weakness because they are unable to ask for help when they do need it. People who are confident and capable can discern the difference between asking for help for every little thing and never asking for help even when it is most desperately needed.

*You need practical help*: you've lost an important file from your hard disk. Say, 'Could you help me? I think I've lost the König file from my hard disk.' Here, you get straight to the point: in a work environment it is inappropriate to ask things in a roundabout way as it wastes the other person's time.

*You need to ask for time* for someone to listen. You know she is very busy and it's hard to find the right moment because she is always in such a hurry. Say, 'Sally, I know you're very busy at the moment but I have a problem and believe you could help. Could we arrange a time so that I could talk to you about it?' Offering to postpone your conversation to a more convenient time for Sally shows that you are not taking her availability for granted.

She may say she has the time there and then, but it is important you have shown consideration for her needs: it makes it more likely that she will be willing to help and it shows that you respect her.

*You need to ask for advice* from a friend about what to do about your partner's dishonesty and infidelity. If you simply state what he has done, your friend won't know that you are asking for advice. If you say, 'What would you do?' you are asking what she would do, not what she thinks you ought to do. Instead say, 'Why do you think this keeps happening? How should I deal with it?' This gives your friend something concrete to work on with you, definite things to discuss such as how many times it's happened and your reaction to each lie and infidelity and the message it has given your partner – such as your being prepared to forgive and forgive and forgive as you've accepted this behaviour in the past.

*You need informational help* from a friend to find out about angina as your daughter has just been diagnosed with it. If you say, 'What do you know about angina?' it does not tell him why you need to know so he may just say, 'Nothing' without probing further; it can also sound interrogative. If you say, 'I've just found out my daughter's got angina but I don't know what that is' you are not directly asking for help, so it is a passive way of asking. Instead say, 'Do you know anything about angina? My daughter's just been told she has it and I don't know what it is.'

*You need to ask for compassionate help* because you are ill and need to go home. An aggressive way of doing this would be to say, 'Why don't *you* go to the conference for a change?' A passive way of asking would be to say, 'Would you like to take my place at the conference?' What you should say, is, 'Could you cover for me at the conference as I don't feel well and would like to go home?' As well as being clear about your needs when asking for help, you must also make sure that you show gratitude when help has been given or offered: 'I really appreciate that. I didn't want the boss to think I was trying to shirk my responsibilities.'

## Asking for forgiveness

*Aggressive people* find it hard to ask for forgiveness because they feel admitting to wanting to be forgiven is showing a sign of weakness. They are also afraid of refusal, fearing they might be ridiculed.

Charles wants to ask forgiveness from Gloria. If he says, 'A mean-minded individual like you doesn't forgive easily' he insults and offends Gloria so she is less likely to feel generous about forgiving him and may fulfil his expectation of her – that of being mean-minded. Charles has shown he does not expect to be forgiven and Gloria, if she were to forgive him now, would have no pleasure in doing so but instead would feel quite bitter towards him. He had not only wounded her once – why he needed forgiveness in the first place – but again by being rude to her when he'd thought he'd asked for forgiveness.

*Passive people* find it hard to ask for forgiveness because they fear it won't be given: rejection would make them feel worse. If Charles says, 'How could you ever forgive me?' he shows he does not expect to be forgiven and would be surprised if he were. This makes it harder for Gloria to be forgiving because it implies she is forgiving against Charles' 'better' judgment.

*Assertive people* are direct and give no hidden messages. Charles could simply say, 'Will you forgive me?' This is a straightforward question with no hidden messages, leaving Gloria to choose whether she does forgive Charles without having to worry about him calling her names or deciding for her whether he deserves forgiveness.

## Asking for important things

When you are asking for something that is very important to you or something that you have a stake in, plan beforehand what you are going to say and how you need to put it: a clumsy attempt may well spoil everything. Even if you don't hold much hope for something that you want, there is still no harm in trying. Think of whom you are asking, and what it is you are asking. If it's a reasonable request, ask the question in such a way as to show that it is reasonable and that you're being reasonable. For example, you need to ask your boss for the next day off even though you're meant to give a week's notice.

| | |
|---|---|
| *You:* | Could I take tomorrow off to go to the passport office? They say they mislaid my forms and unless I can go in person they might not be able to issue my visa in time for my holiday next week. |
| *Employer:* | This is at a very inconvenient time. You know we're behind schedule. |
| *You:* | I'm prepared to stay late tonight and come in early on Wednesday to make up for it. |
| *Employer:* | There won't be any overtime in it. |
| *You:* | I'm still prepared to do it. |
| *Employer:* | OK. But leave more time to get your passport sorted out next time. |
| *You:* | I will. Thank you. |

The request was made more palatable by coming to some mutually agreeable arrangement by you offering to work overtime for nothing. Any agreements must not be made in an underhand or manipulative way: be open about what you need and why; you will be refused outright if the person feels he is being cheated in some way.

Suppose a group of you is planning to go on holiday together in France. The others seem to have made all the arrangements without consulting you but you want to be part of the decision-making team, as you are an equal member of the party. So, you must say what it is that you want. Own your statement by starting with 'I': 'I feel that I haven't been consulted over our plans. All the decisions seem to have been made without discussing them with me. I particularly wanted to visit Angers in the Loire as I have an aunt who lives there. I'm sure she'd be happy to put us up for a couple of nights. It's a lovely city and staying with her could save us a lot of money.' Here, you assertively pointed out the unfairness of not being included in holiday discussions, made your request and told them how it could benefit everyone, not just yourself.

Suppose you want to ask your employer permission to attend a course in office hours – you have arranged a mutually convenient time to do this. Say, 'I'd like to go on a day release course on computer skills at the technical college because I feel we could both benefit if I were better qualified to do the job. I would be of more use to you because I could fill in when Angharad's off sick and I'd feel my job would be more secure.' Here you have shown that your request could benefit you both. Don't try to manipulate your employer by implying she would be the only one to benefit. That ruse is easily seen through and you would come down in her estimation of you.

### Making rules

You are in control of what you do and don't do. To ensure that people realise this you must make the rules. If you want to break these rules occasionally, that is your privilege, but having these rules makes it easier to deal with other people.

*Working rules*. Your colleagues or fellow students need to understand your boundaries. For example, if someone asks to borrow your essay because they hadn't the time say, 'No, I'm sorry Josh. I spent a long time on this and I'm not prepared to lend it to anyone.' Expect the same response if you ask someone else the same question.

*Rules for overlap with others*. These are rules for others to follow if part of their life overlaps or interferes with yours. Suppose you are Jewish and share a house with people from other cultures. It is important that your religious rules are observed and you cannot do that without other people's cooperation. Say, 'Please never borrow any of my cutlery or pans or crockery. I don't want them to be used for any non-kosher food.'

*Lifestyle rules.* If you make it clear from the beginning what your boundaries are it will save you from having to make explanations at a more embarrassing or inconvenient time. For example, it is easier to tell people that you don't drink alcohol so that you are not persuaded to imbibe at every social occasion. This might also be a good idea even if you rarely drink so that you don't have to keep explaining why you are not drinking at this particular time and suffer others trying to persuade you to change your mind.

If men often try to pick you up, it is easier to make it clear from the start that you are not interested because you are married or that you only date other women – or whatever reason applies. If you live a long way out of town and don't travel home on your own when it's late and dark and a friend invites you to see a show after work say, 'I'm sorry but I can't come. I don't travel on public transport late at night on my own' or, 'I'd love to come. Could I spend the night with you as I don't feel safe going home alone late at night?'

# 15

# GIVING SKILFUL CRITICISM

Giving criticism is very important: it gives other people feedback on how they are doing and how you perceive them, and you can use it to change the way people behave towards you and others in general. You can also use it to help change and improve the world around you such as bringing something to light that initiates a change in company or governmental policy. Without criticism, people would not have the incentive or motivation to maintain or improve standards and people would not be aware of any lack in service or how their neglect has affected others.

### Skilful criticism
When you criticise someone, it is important to remain polite and calm. (Also see *Feedback* in Chapter 11, page 123, and *Conflict and complaints* in Chapter 12, page 136.)

*Concentrate on the other person's behaviour* instead of making personal comments, otherwise he will probably focus on the names you've just called him rather than the issue itself. For example, instead of calling your partner disgusting, concentrate on what you object to: 'Could you close your mouth when you eat? It makes me feel ill seeing chewed food in your mouth.' If someone is unkind to you don't say, 'You're unkind', as this is aggressive, but, 'What you've just said is very unkind.' Here, you haven't labelled the whole person – as in the aggressive response – but the person's behaviour at that time.

*Be prepared to back up your criticism* with an example – and preferably with a suggestion of how things can be put right. If you don't give that example when criticising, you can expect the other person to ask for one.

*Own what you say* by starting your sentences with 'I'. Instead of saying, 'There's a pair of jeans soaking in the bath' say, 'I need to have a bath but there are some jeans in it. Are they yours?'

*Be specific with the criticism* to aid understanding and show that you respect the other person enough to make clear what the problem is. Instead of saying, 'There have been too many mistakes recently . . .' say, 'I noticed that the last proposal form you handed in lacked . . .' Then the other person can focus on what you're saying without trying to puzzle over what you're getting at.

*Be specific with how you feel* so that the other person can understand exactly what it is she has done to upset you. For example, your teenage daughter treats your home like a hotel. She expects meals on the table when she comes home – if she comes home – and her washing gathered from the floor of different rooms. She then expects it to be washed and ironed and replaced in her wardrobe ready for the next time she wants to wear it. Tell her what you don't like and then say, 'It saddens me that you treat me and your home with such a marked lack of respect and it saddens me that I have to talk to you in this way.'

Here, your daughter knows exactly what she's done wrong, what has upset you and how you feel. She now has the opportunity to tell you how she views the mentioned problems and whether she is prepared to try to change her ways.

*Get the timing right* or the point you want to make will be lost. Someone who has just got home from a tiring day, for example, won't want to listen to complaints and is likely to answer back aggressively; then you will have achieved nothing. Wait until he has had time to relax and you have exchanged greetings and asked how each other's day went. Then you can gauge whether it is the right time at all to bring up the subject.

It is also important to give the criticism immediately, not a month after, for example, you were shown a presentation. Waiting this long shows a lack of respect and suggests you have not taken the other person seriously – she may well not take you seriously either and ignore your comments.

*Give criticism earlier rather than later* as it is easier to put right before it becomes an ingrained habit. Early feedback also reduces the stress of having to put up with it for a long time and means that you can tell the person calmly about it rather than waiting until you can't take any more, exploding in anger and frustration.

Also, don't choose criticisms that are past their date. For example, if you are criticised for a regular habit, it is pointless to bring it to your partner's attention that three years ago he was doing something similar. If it annoyed you, you should have mentioned it at the time, not wait three years to dredge it up.

*Be constructive and selective* by suggesting how to put a few things right without completely destroying the other person's confidence (also see *Prioritising criticism* on page 168). For example, you have a clumsy friend who walks into things, drops things, frequently trips up and lets things boil over on the cooker. When she washes up, her clothes and the floor are soaked and when she baths, the floor gets wet and slippery. Since you do not want to crush your friend with what you say, decide which aspect of her clumsiness is most worrying. Then think up a careful comment on how this affects you and what she might be able to do to improve the situation: 'Nancy, I've noticed that when you have a bath or wash up, water gets spilt over the floor which we all step into. I'm worried about this as it could be quite dangerous, especially in the kitchen. It might be a good idea only to fill the sink and bath half full.'

*Be gentle:* it is sometimes useful to play down a criticism so that it does not come across as a formal complaint. When my daughter's school bus regularly failed to display the children on board sign it was legally obliged to, I decided to have a quiet word with the driver instead of complaining to the company direct for both the driver's sake and for the sake of good relations between him and my daughter as he was likely to be in regular contact with her. I said, 'Excuse me, could I have a chat about something? I didn't want to ring the bus company; I thought it better to mention it to you. Do you realise that the children on board sign often isn't displayed? I understand it's a legal requirement for school buses and I'm concerned about the children's safety.'

I didn't directly blame the driver – although displaying the sign was his responsibility – and I achieved my aim without causing hostility. Showing sensitivity like this may well reap rewards that a direct complaint to the company would not. Both methods may get the same result – the sign being displayed. But one may cause animosity while the other does not.

Gentle criticism is best used if the issue itself is sensitive or if you are regularly going to have contact with that person again. Or you may just be a gentle, tactful person who prefers a sensitive approach. Sometimes a gentle touch on the other person's arm will help temper what you say so that the message is even more gentle.

### Inappropriate criticism

There is often no need to criticise at all, yet many people simply can't help giving their opinion. You don't get the best out of people when you show your negative thoughts unless the other person can see the need for you to have said what you have, and you are constructive where possible.

*Suspend judgment* on moral issues: it is easy to make snap judgments when you're not the other person; you haven't had his life experience, got his personality or had his temptations and opportunities.

Suppose your friend's brother is in hospital, very ill, with breathing problems and problems with blood clots in his legs. Don't say, 'That's poetic justice for someone who's been a heavy smoker all his life. What did he expect?' It serves no purpose to tell your friend that his brother's illness was smoking induced: she would already know. You can't make her brother better by telling her your negative opinion – however much you may personally feel it is well founded. Instead, be supportive: 'I'm so sorry. You must be feeling dreadfully worried. It must be awful to see him suffering.' If your friend smokes too, you might want to say gently: 'I'm very worried that *you* smoke and I wish you didn't. Would you consider giving up? I wouldn't want the same thing to happen to you.'

*Don't presume to know what you don't* – it is easy to criticise without understanding the whole situation. If, for example, you find out a friend is pregnant, you need to find out how she feels about it before you criticise or congratulate her. Don't say, 'You idiot' or, 'You've let your mum down' but say, 'Is that what you want?' or, 'Do I congratulate or commiserate?' or, 'How do you feel about it?' Take the rest of your cues from her.

### Prioritising criticism

If you pick on every little thing to criticise you lose credibility when you make an issue of something worth making a fuss about. You will also risk getting a reputation for nagging, being unreasonable, unapproachable and over-critical, never having anything positive to say.

*Prioritise criticism in teaching*: don't pick up on every small misdemeanour children and young adults in your care make or they may become disaffected with the educational environment and have difficulty relating to adults in authority. It is possible to be strict and fair, without being overbearing, retaining pupils' respect for you. Valuable lesson time would be lost in bringing every minor incident to the attention of the culprit. Also, if a major incident then occurs you have few remaining strictures, as most, or all, sanctions would have already been used making the punishment less effective.

Have a clear scale of unacceptable behaviour in your mind. For minor incidents, all that is needed might be a raised eyebrow, hands on hips or a raised voice. For a pupil chewing gum, a pointing finger indicating the rubbish bin would not interrupt the flow of the lesson.

In challenging classes, teachers lower their expectations of behaviour in order to keep the lesson moving forward, so retaining the concentration of the majority of the class. It is always possible to mention minor misdemeanours to the individuals concerned at the end of the lesson where the discussion would not cause disruption and reduces the risk of serious confrontation with the rest of the class as an interested audience.

*Prioritise criticism in an office*: don't address every little mistake; concentrate on staff members' strengths rather than weaknesses, to motivate them. When you do criticise, ensure that it is an important matter and that you have your facts right before you make an issue of the event. Also, look at the overall picture of the person's work: balance criticism to show that you have noticed the good as well as the bad. You may feel that the good far outweighs the bad so that some minor transgressions are best ignored to preserve goodwill. For example, if an employee regularly comes in to work ten minutes late, should she be reprimanded? What you do may depend on how vital timekeeping is for the type of work she does, the quality of her work and how hard she works.

If punctual timekeeping is not vital, her work is very good and she often works through her lunch hour and remains behind after work hours without overtime pay, you may decide not to mention her tardiness. You may not gain anything by pointing out the lack of a mere ten minutes at the start of the day as you risk her extending her reformed timekeeping to the lunch hours and evenings as well, and take every break owing to her. You would then, as an employer, have lost out. If, however, as well as arriving late she took extended lunch breaks and left five minutes before time at the end of the day, you might think her timekeeping well worth mentioning, before she takes further advantage of a non-vigilant management.

*Prioritise criticism as a parent*: don't continually criticise your children as that makes them feel bad about themselves and does not encourage good behaviour. Give warning of any punishments for repeated offences: 'If you do that again I'll switch off the television' and give your child a chance to modify her behaviour: 'If you still want to go out tonight, I suggest you tidy your room/do your homework now' or, 'If you don't hurry we won't have time for that game of chess.'

*Prioritise criticism as a partner*: pick on one thing at a time, starting with the habit that annoys you most or that has the worst consequences, and be ready to receive similar criticism about yourself – not as retaliation but as the natural course of communicating between you and your partner. He may say, 'As we are on the subject of annoying habits, there's something you do I'd like to mention . . .'

*Don't be unduly destructive*: there is no need to dash a person's confidence completely by telling her all there is to know about what she is doing wrong. Pick on one or two important issues and explain what it is she is doing wrong and how she can put things right. For example, your student friend has just been warned that she may fail the course. She is very upset and comes to you for advice. You need to choose advice from the following list in order to help her:

- Don't stay up all night socialising.
- Don't get drunk on a regular basis.
- Don't skip lectures.
- Don't keep copying my work, do it yourself.
- Work when you have a free hour or two between lectures instead of drinking coffee and chatting.
- Use the library.
- Don't join so many activities.
- Don't go home on the weekends, stay in college and study.
- Attend tutorials.

An aggressive way of criticising is to tell your friend all of the things she, in your opinion, is doing wrong. She is then likely to be more upset because you have, in her eyes, just set her an impossible task and too many truths are uncomfortable. It would also make you sound very goody-goody and judgmental which is liable to build barriers between you. Being so used to her way of life, completely changing it might prove too much of a task. A passive way of criticising is not to offer any constructive criticism at all but just to reassure her that she'll do fine in the end if she works a little harder.

An assertive response to your friend's cry for help may be to say, 'Why don't you try to be more organised by planning what you need to do each week to meet the deadlines? If you go to bed earlier you'll be more refreshed and work more productively. You know, it hasn't helped you to copy my work. Why don't you try it yourself and then I'll help you with the bits you get stuck on?' Then, as time goes on, you could add, 'It really helps if you take your own notes at the lectures instead of borrowing someone else's. They don't mean nearly as much as when you write them down yourself. And it helps you to remember what was said when you come to revise.' And so on.

# 16

# HANDLING CRITICISM AND WORK BULLIES

Being criticised is unpleasant. You'd like to think of yourself as doing well but as soon as someone criticises you, you know you've fallen short of your ideal and that others know it too. This embarrasses you and temporarily lowers your self-esteem. But whether it lowers your self-esteem in the long run depends on what you do with the knowledge of your mistakes. You might deny that you've done wrong or try to put the blame on someone else – when inside you know the fault was yours and that you should have been big enough to own up to it – or you might accept whatever blame is yours and consider it a learning experience for the future.

Regular unfair criticism and other inappropriate behaviour from others in the work place amounts to work bullying, and needs particular care.

### Value of criticism
Criticism serves a useful purpose: it gives you feedback on how you are doing (see *Feedback* in Chapter 11, page 123) and without it you would very often not be able to see where you have gone wrong and in what way. Criticism allows you to guard against the same mistake in the future.

For example, when you are at home, you have a habit of singing your favourite songs out of tune. You do this so often you're quite unaware when you break into song. It all sounds fine to you so when there are guests in the house you think nothing of it. If no one tells you what a dreadful singer you are, you would embarrass yourself when significant people in your life are near you. If someone does tell you that you can't sing in tune, and she even offers to prove it by recording your singing, she may have done you a favour. You can then be aware of what you sound like and limit your singing to when you're alone – or get lessons!

If you are unemployed and regularly go for job interviews without success, you need to know why. Is it because of some lack over which you have no control or is it because of your performance at the interview? Or perhaps you are going for a job or career that is unsuited to you and your talents. Might you need to change direction? It is far better to learn these things early on in your search for a job rather than be disappointed a hundred times over, making you feel despondent and angry. Unemployment affects the entire family: you have a right to ask about your perceived shortcomings and your personal value makes asking worthwhile.

### Responding to criticism

It's very easy to be aggressive when someone criticises you because you are immediately on the defensive, ready to protect your ground, or passive in that you don't know how to respond. But listen to what is said, without reacting with your emotions, before carefully considering your response. If your partner says the gravy you made is rather lumpy, an aggressive reply would be, 'Well, I've not noticed that yours is any better.' A passive reply would be, 'I'm terrible at cooking' and an assertive response would be, 'It is. Sorry.'

If your neighbour asks when you are going to cut your grass as your lawn is making the rest of the small street look unkempt an aggressive reply would be, 'Your garden's hardly going to win any awards.' A passive reply would be, 'Oh, I've been meaning to cut it. I'll get round to it' and an assertive response would be, 'You're right. My lawn does need cutting. I'll do it at the weekend.'

*Clarify the criticism* if it is given in an unclear way so that you can best judge how you are to reply: the person will have to justify his comment with an example.

*Person:*     You don't know what faithful means!

*Response:*   What are you getting at?

*Person:*     I saw you in the pub last night talking to a man with dark hair. You told me Barry is blond.

*Response:*   Seeing me with someone other than my partner does not mean I am unfaithful. And I don't need to explain myself to you. Barry knows where I was and who with.

*Is the criticism fair?* Accept what is fair and reject what is not. If only half of what was said was fair, explain which part you accept and deny the other part, giving proof. Suppose someone tells you that you are not a good Catholic because, although you always attend mass on Sundays, you miss the Holy Days of Obligation. You could say, 'That doesn't mean I'm not a good Catholic. It means I'm not good at attending Holy Days of Obligation. And I don't think you're in a position to judge: only God can do that.'

Someone tells you that you lead an unhealthy lifestyle because you drink alcohol and smoke. You could say, 'It is unhealthy to smoke, and to drink to excess. But I eat very little fatty food, have plenty of fresh fruit and vegetables and exercise three times a week. On balance I'm probably more healthy than you.'

Someone says, 'You're lazy. Why don't you get a job like

other people?' You could say, 'I'd love to have a job, but like with many other people, it hasn't been possible. Are you in a position to offer me one? I'm available right now.'

*Accept responsibility for your mistakes* immediately and ask how you can put the matter right. Denying things that are true fools no one, and makes you feel very uncomfortable the next time you see that person or anyone else in the know about what you did.

Suppose you put your partner's white shirt in a dark wash by mistake and it came out grey. He told you that he would do his own washing in future, as you couldn't be trusted to follow the basic rules of the washing machine. You could say, 'I'm sorry. It was careless of me. You have every right to be angry.'

If you are criticised by a friend for making a flippant comment about the unemployed – you had forgotten that his partner has been unemployed for years – you could say, 'I'm sorry. That was tactless of me' or, 'I'm sorry. That came out all wrong. I hadn't thought it through.' Apologising restores pride to the person whose feelings you have just hurt. If you let the mistake stand you would feel bad about it afterwards.

*Make amends.* If you need to own up to something or apologise, do it as soon as possible, but not when, for example, the person is busy, has had bad news or there is a crisis in the office. Wait until he is calm and more likely to be able to listen to you properly. In the example above where you ruined your partner's shirt you could offer to buy a new one: 'Let me make it up to you by buying you a new shirt.'

### Dealing with work bullies

People bully because they feel insecure about their abilities and are envious of others. Bullying is aggressive behaviour and is usually carried out by people in positions of authority. If you are a bully, you will not be thought highly of and, if you are bullied, you need to do something to rescue yourself from the situation as it can seriously affect your health.

## Standing up to work bullies

Work bullies' attacks tend to be verbal or through body language, although some include physical violence and sexual assault. The sooner you recognise a bully, the sooner you can put things right. A bullying person can:

- Overreact to small mistakes you make.
- Humiliate you in front of others at work.
- Never take on board your suggestions: or later follow them through but fail to give you the credit.
- Be sarcastic.
- Either overload you with work or not give you enough to do.
- Be deliberately awkward when you need time off, including your annual leave.
- Scrutinise everything you do to find fault, yet not do the same with others in the department.
- Report you for something that hasn't been discussed with you beforehand and with no warning.
- Bring forward deadlines at short notice to make you look incompetent if you finish late.
- Ask you to make the coffee or tea when it's definitely not your job to do so.
- Be very quick to blame you if something goes wrong without first trying to establish all the facts.

When dealing with bullies stay calm – do not give the bully the pleasure of seeing you riled – and don't respond to personal comments by firing back equally offensive comments or by being sarcastic as these only make the situation worse. Concentrate on each comment as it is made: if there is anything with which you disagree challenge the bully to show you won't be pushed around. Ensure you tackle the issue brought up rather than address a past grievance.

Ensure you meet the bully's gaze with an erect posture and face him squarely, look serious, and sound confident – your voice should be firm and steady.

If a male colleague repeatedly makes racist and sexist jokes in your hearing that you find offensive (also see Chapter 18), you could say, 'I thought this company was meant to be an equal opportunities employer, yet your jokes are about discrimination.' If he carries on, write down what he says and take it to the personnel officer or your boss. If he is your boss you will need to challenge him assertively and remind him about equality in the work place – or go to his boss.

Suppose your boss often incorrectly implies you are late with your work and says, 'Haven't you finished that report yet?' even though the deadline is three days ahead. You could say, 'No. I understood the deadline is not for another three days' or, 'Do you need it ahead of schedule? I understood I had another three days.'

Suppose your boss often implies that you are struggling with your work and says, 'You're not still fiddling with those figures are you?' You could say, 'Are you saying my work is too slow?' or, 'I'm glad you noticed, I'm having difficulty with it. Could you explain how this is meant to work?' Your boss has just given himself a job to do.

You find that your boss always finds fault with whatever work you do. The latest comment is, 'That's not how I set it out.' You could say, 'Is there something wrong with my layout?' Just because you've done it differently does not mean that it is wrong. Or you could say, 'Would you like me to change the layout? If you show me your layout, I'm sure it wouldn't take me too long to move things round.' Here, you make the point that your boss had not asked you to lay it out in a certain way: you don't know what the other layout looks like. You're also making the point that it will inevitably take more time, which wastes the company's money if it's unnecessary. Or you could say, 'I didn't know you wanted it set out in a certain way.' It was your boss's responsibility to give full clear instructions and you have pointed out it was not your mistake: she may even apologise for not having told you the layout was crucial. Or your boss may admit to it not mattering: which would make her sound petty for making the comment in the first place.

Be calm while you challenge the criticism in a reasonable way. If the bully doesn't soon stop picking on you, keep a diary of events and get witnesses to comments made or behaviour seen – and write down who these people are next to the relevant entry in your diary – and go to someone in authority for help. Get help from a previous victim if you can. Alternatively, change your job.

### Sexual harassment

Sexual harassment is to do with unsolicited and unwanted sexual attention, usually from the opposite sex – it is more common for men to sexually harass women. It is designed to undermine confidence and to give amusement to those directly involved or to those observing the situation. It can involve too-close physical proximity, touching, physical or sexual assault – the extreme being rape – sexual innuendoes, jokes, comments on someone's appearance, a spread of gossip and offensive 'sex' talk in the person's hearing. It also involves the use of pin-ups and pornographic pictures.

Sexual harassment is bullying and needs to be dealt with head on. Suppose a man at work has told the others in the office he slept with you and that you were really 'easy'. Both are untrue. You could say, 'Why have you told people I slept with you when you know I haven't?' and follow on with, 'This is sexual harassment. Either you tell everyone it was a lie or I'll report you to personnel.'

The start of sexual harassment can be so subtle that you don't realise it is happening until far down the line: you may have thought that an invitation to join someone for drinks after work was just a friendly gesture, especially if it started with a group of people and then you later found yourself going alone with just one of them. And if that person is your boss, how you handle it can affect your prospects within the company and perhaps your reference should you decide to leave.

Suppose your boss invites you to have a drink with him after work, but once there he overtly flirts with you and you realise that you may have given him the false impression that you were interested in him by accepting the invitation. Use body language to show you don't wish to sit too close: move away immediately he gets too close or go to the toilet and, when you come back, seat yourself opposite him. Shorten the time you spend there by quickly finishing your drink and saying you have to go; you could say you are going out with your partner – unless you have already admitted you were free that evening or that you don't have a partner.

If you are direct and say you have no interest in a personal relationship with him, it may affect your career prospects. Bosses tend to have the upper hand. It is probably better at this stage to keep your distance and write down anything concrete that happens and if anyone witnessed it; it will help if you need to make a formal complaint. You cannot effectively complain against being made to feel uncomfortable. However, if your boss makes a deliberate pass at you by putting a hand on your thigh: state calmly and clearly that you are leaving and do so, complain to your personnel officer or your boss's boss and tell your union. It is also useful to find out if he has behaved like this with other people. If an assault takes place, you should complain to the police.

**The impact of bullying and sexual harassment**
The effect on victims' lives following bullying or sexual harassment can be immense and enduring. If you are

bullied you can lose confidence and self-esteem, become depressed and withdrawn, not wanting to mix with people outside work at all, and be so overwhelmed by your problems that you are unable to hold a conversation about anything apart from what's happening at work. The effect on you may be so great that you lose your job and become unable to get or hold down another. You may become phobic about going to work and be physically sick in the mornings and/or suffer from panic attacks – and you may be at risk of committing suicide.

Needing vast amounts of support over a long period affects the whole family.

Avenues of help include the company's complaints procedure, your union, the Citizens Advice Bureau (the phone number is in your telephone directory), and your doctor – you may be able to get time off work to sort out what to do, to give you a break if you badly need it or to arrange counselling. You could seek help from a solicitor and consider taking legal action against the bully, or seek help from a body that is set up to help victims of work bullying and sexual harassment.

If you have tried to handle a bully without any measure of success and there is no support for you in the company, it is best to look for somewhere else to work. You could have an interview with the personnel officer the day you leave and be very frank about what has been going on so that the company is made aware of the type of employee it has.

# 17

# DEALING WITH GENERAL PUT-DOWNS

Put-down comments are designed to make you feel small and bad about yourself, are always unfair or unreasonably unkind in some way and must be challenged to protect yourself against bullying tactics even if it is just to politely put the other person in her place.

Many people don't realise that they regularly put people down, perhaps because they are arrogant and have an over-inflated opinion of themselves, or because they don't think highly of others or don't care whom they hurt. Some people just have poor social skills and don't think before they speak.

## Responding to general put-downs

*An aggressive response* to a put-down might be to make a sharp comment, start a fight or to take subtle revenge by starting malicious rumours about the person.

*A passive response* to a put-down might be to harbour a grudge long after the event; possibly long after the person who made the comment had forgotten he'd ever said it. You might never use any form of reproach but, long into the future, when he is in need of help and you are the one person who is able to give it, you might refuse that help –

and he wouldn't know why unless you chose to tell him.

*An assertive response* to a put-down would be to challenge it: this could be done by questioning its validity, by pointing out how rude the person is to have said such a thing or to point out she is misinformed.

If you are stuck for an assertive reply use a general response such as: 'Do you get a buzz out of making me feel small?' or, 'Why did you say that?' or, 'That was a very judgmental thing to say.'

### Obvious put-downs

Obvious put-downs include saying: 'Is that all you can manage?' or, 'Get a life of your own!' or, 'Can't you do better than that?' But sometimes, the put-down is achieved through body language: sneering and showing disgust (you're stupid or this is the stupidest idea), laughing derisively (you're pathetic, is that all you can manage?), and loudly sighing while folding arms and raising eyes to the ceiling (this is going to take all day and he's already bored by it). You could respond to any of these put-downs by saying, 'Is there a problem?'

Challenge obvious put-downs head on. For example, you take a cake that you made into work to share between your friends and one of them laughs and says, 'Is it worth the risk? We've got the AGM [Annual General Meeting] tomorrow and can't be off with food poisoning.' You could say, 'What you have just said is both rude and unkind. If you don't want a slice, Jasmine, just say, "No thank you." '

Suppose you have very bad acne and someone says, 'Hey, did you just land from the planet Spot?' You could say, 'That was a very cruel thing to say. I wouldn't feel proud of myself for saying something like that. Does it make you feel you're better than I am?'

Suppose you had to make an outfit for your son's performance at a school play. You hate making things and found this job a real burden. When you are at school, getting your son ready for the performance, someone laughs at your attempt and says, 'What on earth's that meant to be?' You could say, 'It's an elf costume, Maggie. I hope you haven't hurt Stuart's feelings because you've certainly hurt mine.'

I don't read books in the normal way because I have a problem with my hands; it hurts me to grip anything for a long time, so I joined Listening Books. Someone once said to me, 'That's the lazy way to read' and I resented it because I felt it implied I was lazy, so I said, 'It's nice to read books without having to hold them and turn pages as it hurts my hands, but I wouldn't call myself lazy.'

*Sarcasm* can be dealt with by responding to the comment at face value and ignoring any innuendo. For example, if you are a mature student who usually gets no more than a C despite working hard, and your tutor says to you, 'Is this up to your usual high standard?' you could say, 'I did my best as I always do.' This is a straightforward response, ignoring the tutor's implication that your work is usually below standard. Or if you came last in the London Marathon and an acquaintance says nastily, 'Well done! You came last! You must tell me how you do it', say, 'It's unkind of you to make fun. My purpose was not to win but to take part. I don't need to be first to enjoy running and raising money for charity.' Here you have made your point that the person was unnecessarily cruel. You have also pointed out that his priorities are wrong.

**Subtle put-downs**
Some put-downs are hard to detect, especially for outsiders, which makes it harder for the person using the putdown to be discovered at being underhand or unkind. Suppose you have been chronically ill for some time but have not had much sympathy or understanding. You know you look awful and someone who privately detests you

says in front of everyone, 'It's so nice to see you looking so well now' implying that when you don't look well you must look very rough indeed or that, as you look well you must be feeling well and are therefore malingering. Say, 'Thank you. I'm glad I don't look as bad as I feel' or, 'Really? What makes you think I look so well today?' If you really do look how you feel, it would be hard for the person to justify her comment and she would lose face.

Subtle put-down body language can be carried out in such a way that only you notice so the person's character is preserved in the minds of others while he makes you look or feel stupid with the minimum of effort or thought. It can include: a gaze to the ceiling – this is boring; a slight raising of an eyebrow – I think you are lying; a hint of a smile – I've got an advantage over you; a slight look of surprise – it's unlike you to achieve anything worthwhile; the gentle rubbing of a forefinger against a temple – you are about to do something stupid, and a slight scratching of the head – what you are saying is somewhat confused.

Either ignore subtle put-downs or challenge them head on. If you do challenge them, don't pretend you do not understand the message you are given. For example, you have to explain something complicated to a new member of staff in the presence of your colleague who knows all about it and raises her gaze to the ceiling looking bored. You could say, 'I know you're very familiar with this, Karen, but Terry's hearing it for the first time. Next time you can explain the process to the new recruit.' Or when you ask someone in your office for help and she smirks as though to say you are stupid, say, 'Is your smirk a "Yes, you will help me?" or a "No, I won't?" '

*Crumple buttons* are spots of vulnerability that, when touched, can elicit a big emotional response. Be careful to whom you reveal your 'crumple button'. (The examples below are not intended to suggest you should never confide in anyone.)

Suppose you tell someone in confidence that, because of cancer, you've had an early hysterectomy and are extremely sad that you can't have children. But when you are socialising with a large group of people this person deliberately steers the conversation round to babies and pregnancies, safe in the knowledge that you won't publicly criticise her as that would involve revealing your medical history to all present. Try and change the direction of the conversation so that you won't have to suffer for long; after the event, tell the person what you think of her behaviour: 'I felt very hurt Friday evening when you initiated the conversation about babies. It was very insensitive of you and I very much regret telling you about not being able to have children of my own.'

Suppose you tell someone in confidence that you were abused as a child and one thing you cannot stand is someone stroking the back of your neck as that makes you relive memories of what the person used to do. Your confidant later says, in front of others, what a lovely neck you have and asks if they agree. The attention of everyone looking at your neck tremendously upsets you. You know that no genuine compliment by this person was intended: he said it to make you feel small and bad about yourself. You could cut the attention by saying, 'Can we leave my neck alone now? It's embarrassing me' or just briefly thank them for their kind words and change the subject yourself. If it is a subject that would be of genuine interest to the others the switch in conversation will look slick and no one else will know that you felt uncomfortable.

### Self put-downs
Sometimes people put themselves down by showing weaknesses or vulnerable areas to others who may be unscrupulous with the knowledge they have been given by repeating what was said to someone else. For example, if you are cashing up in the bank where you work and drop a pile of

change on the floor, don't say, 'How clumsy of me. I do this all the time' but, 'Have you seen any of my money roll over your way?' Cast no judgmental comments on yourself. For your boss to overhear or later be told that you regularly drop your money on the floor would not help your promotional prospects.

Sometimes, people put themselves down to make someone else feel better. You might say to someone whose cake collapsed on removal from the oven, 'I'm useless at baking. Any cake of mine would have fared no better. Don't worry about it.' However, putting yourself down to make someone else feel better is not a positive thing to do: continually belittling yourself shows others how little you think of yourself, which will make them wonder about your personal worth too. Instead, think of helpful things to say without mentioning your lack of attributes such as, 'Never mind. It'll still taste good.' You can also share genuine experiences. For example, you could say, 'That happened to me once. It still tasted good.' Here you are not putting yourself down but stating that you understand how it feels, showing common ground. (In Japan and China, it is considered positive to be modest and self-effacing and in efforts to appear modest the Japanese and Chinese put themselves and other family members down to put guests at ease.)

### Be prepared

If you know you have a vulnerable area that someone is likely to pick on, prepare yourself for the eventuality in advance by, for example, considering what has been said to you in the past and working out what you could have said to protect yourself assertively – if you deal with these things aggressively you risk the other person knowing she has scored by touching a raw nerve: you are also seen to be a 'prickly pear'. Then remember these prepared responses for the next time the same, or similar, comments are made to you.

Where possible, find out as much as you can about your vulnerable situation. For example, if you have gone for a job you didn't get, find out the level of competition – such as how many applicants there were – so that you can use the information in your response. So when someone says, 'I didn't think you'd get that job' you can say, 'The odds were against me as there were a hundred and twenty applicants but I didn't let the likely popularity of the job put me off from trying.' If someone says, 'Unemployed people are lazy' you could say, 'It's easy to generalise about the unemployed, particularly when you are employed yourself.' Or if someone says, 'You can't be up to much if you've not got a job' you could say, 'I don't have a job at the moment but that does not mean I have no worth. Economic changes and boardroom politics are out of my control. Being made redundant is common-place and happens to many a previously valued worker.'

### Take responsibility for what you say

If someone has already had many bad things said about her and you then put her down, her already poor self-esteem will become even lower – and she is more likely fully to believe what you say. The one put-down you give will result in the person having much lower self-esteem than is warranted by a single comment in isolation: so be careful if you use a put-down, as you have no idea what has been said to the person in the past. What you might think is a comment to cause minor damage might actually cause cataclysmic damage: it might be the final push towards, for example, a suicide attempt. Although you might not be held responsible for the actual act, if you have contributed to someone's emotional pain – especially, for example, through long-term bullying – you would feel very guilty if that person were to later end her life because of what had been said and done to her.

A dangerous area of attack is talking about someone's

size or appearance. A careless remark – or a well-aimed one – may have far-reaching effects. If, for example, you tell someone she is fat either because you wish to hurt her or because you envy her beautiful curvy body – and you are the hundredth person who has said this – you can expect the person to do something about it. She may need to prove to herself and others she is beautiful, although she already is, through excessive dieting, purging (using laxatives) and vomiting. Once someone has an eating disorder, it is very hard to change the person's way of thinking in order for her to eat normally again. It might take years or it might not be possible at all. Bear in mind some men also suffer eating disorders.

If you use put-downs, look to your own life to see what is wrong and why you feel the need to use them. Generally, happy and fulfilled individuals do not need to boost their egos through negative behaviour towards others.

# 18

# DEALING WITH PREJUDICIAL AND STEREOTYPICAL PUT-DOWNS

Put-downs based on prejudice and stereotyping may be harder to deal with than general put-downs as your response must not only challenge what was said but also the hidden implications based on years, or even a lifetime, of ignorance and false learning. And to do that while remaining assertive is often hard to do, but it is the most effective way to deal with such put-downs.

### Prejudices

Prejudice is having a previous opinion as to whether you like something or someone without any true knowledge of the thing or person. An example of having a previous opinion without knowledge is saying that a certain food is disgusting, without having ever tried it – and you can only say that you don't like the look or smell of it, if you've had a chance to see or smell it.

With prejudicial put-downs, the prejudice is often directed at people and their behaviour. If someone says to you, 'I don't like people who are gay' say, 'How many gay people do you know? Have you met any?' or, 'Why don't you like them?'

Imagine a friend asks if you could meet him in town but you say you have to sign on first at the Job Centre. He replies that you haunt the seediest of places even though he's never been there. Say, 'Are you referring to the building or the people who go there? I'm one of them, as you well know.'

Imagine you want to have a party and invite all your friends but someone says to you not to invite your Asian friend as she's not allowed to go to parties and, even if she were, she wouldn't be much fun as she doesn't drink. Say, 'I can see you don't know Kanta very well. I find her company very amusing and she doesn't need to have a drink first to make her so. I want to invite her whether she's allowed to come or not.'

To be respected in the adult world, prejudices had better be left unspoken even if you can't avoid thinking them.

### Stereotyping

Stereotyping is believing that certain attributes and faults apply to certain groups of people – without exception. These unfounded beliefs are often exaggerated and many of them are based on prejudice. Suppose you're a black African and someone says, 'I'm surprised you can't run any faster. I thought that all you blacks were fast runners.' You could reply, 'It's true that, anatomically, we have the advantage in running because we have a larger heel bone than other races which allows us to push against the ground more forcefully. However, we are not *all* fast runners.'

David is one of eight siblings. Frequently when he meets people and they learn he is from such a large family they ask if he is Catholic. David says, 'Actually, I'm Jewish. But it wasn't a religious decision to have so many children that my parents made; they simply love children and had the financial means to support us all.'

### Racism

Racism is believing your race or ethnic group is superior to others. This belief may be fed by prejudice and stereotyping. For example, you may believe that being white British is superior to being black because you have heard black people are lazy. This is being racist as you feel your race is superior to theirs (and they are, in fact, of many races and have many cultures within those races). It is stereotyping because you are grouping all black people together without exception, and you are prejudiced because this opinion is not based on fact.

Being racist is not going to get you very far if your boss – whose nationality is very different from yours – knows about it. It is also not at all 'politically correct'. You now live in a multicultural society and need to accept it is inappropriate to discriminate in any way. Racist people can be considered biased, ignorant, intolerant, narrow-minded, opinionated, shallow and stubborn.

Suppose you are Jewish and someone at work accuses Jewish people of being mean, in your hearing. You can get out your copy of *The Big Issue* and say, 'I take it that you support deserving causes including the person who sells these outside in the street?' or, 'What evidence do you have to support your view that I'm mean?' If the person can't give evidence you can add, 'Then you know not all Jewish people are mean. Don't you think your statement rather inaccurate?' or, 'It's inaccurate to make such sweeping statements. I don't base my judgment of Gentiles on one or two incidences.' (People often notice evidence that supports their prejudices and ignore evidence that doesn't, so that they can justify their racist stance to themselves.)

You're Muslim and you have chosen not to drink alcohol. The men you go to the pub with tell you you're not really one of the group. Say, 'I thought our friendship was based on how well we relate to each other, not on whether I drink. I feel it's a shame you cannot see past superficialities.'

### Sexism

Sexism is about putting people down because of their sex. Sexist comments against women are designed to 'keep women in their place' and includes: denying women power, assuming they are unable to make important decisions for themselves and that they are incapable of making rational judgments; denying women a wage similar to that of a man working in the same job at the same level; expecting a woman to be at home, busy in the kitchen and bringing up children; expecting a woman, who works the same hours as her male partner, also to cope with the housework and raising of children; expecting it always to be the woman who gives up work to look after young children rather than her male partner; expecting women to be soft and feminine, easily persuaded by the 'stronger' (male) sex; discouraging lesbianism, and punishing women for being sexually experienced ('You slag/slut/whore').

Sexist comments about men are designed to force men into 'machismo' – for men to behave like 'men' and includes: expecting men always to be in control, have power and be strong; discouraging men from displaying emotion (unless it is anger), from crying or from showing sensitivity; discouraging homosexuality and putting down a man who shows characteristics that are stereotypically women's ('Don't be such an old woman'); encouraging men to keep their 'women' under their thumb, and expecting men to be virile and sexually experienced.

Sexist people reward others for remaining in their stereotypes and give penalties to those who don't. But saying, 'She's such a good wife to my son. Her house is something to be proud of. You never see a speck of dust,' has no bearing on whether she is a good wife – it may even show signs of obsessive-compulsive disorder. She may be fussy about the state of her house but shout unremittingly at her children and husband to keep it that way.

Giving advice to a man whose wife does not have the same home-making priorities as in the previous example, another man might say, 'You should take a leaf out of José's book and make her see sense. He's had lots of experience with women and knows how to treat them.' This shows approval of José's insensitive treatment of women and encourages the man to devalue his wife and disregard her needs.

Penalties for non-stereotypical behaviour include calling homosexual women dykes (which implies they have masculine characteristics and are not feminine). The term dyke may also be used to imply a woman is of masculine appearance or behaves in a masculine way. People call homosexual men names such as fairy and poof – names that relate to being female, using the idea of femininity in men insulting. Bi-sexuals fare no better.

There is often little tolerance in society of men and women behaving outside their stereotypical sexual descriptions: if a man displays sensitivity or over-gesticulates, he may be called a pansy; when a woman wears what is accepted as non-feminine clothes with the absence of make-up, she may be described as lesbian. It seems hard for society to accept people as they are without labelling them and making judgments. The more politically correct euphemism for homosexuality is 'same gender oriented' or SGO for short. There is no accompanying criticism or critical emotion associated with this term; it is factual.

Other sexist attitudes include men denying a woman means no when she says no, implying she cannot make decisions for herself and that she does not know her own mind – it is also an excuse for a man to rape a woman known to him ('date rape'), and believing that all women want out of life is to marry, have a home, a husband and children – this is no longer true for the majority of women just as it is not true for the majority of men.

# 19

# ROMANTIC RELATIONSHIPS

Some people are happy on their own and prefer to keep it that way, but many would like to meet someone special with whom to share their life, either temporarily or permanently. The degrees of involvement from a mere acquaintance to a deep and rewarding friendship are many and allow for differences of opinion and interests, but with a romantic relationship both sides may have strong views on personal qualities they are looking for and so can quickly write off another person before giving him or her a chance to be recognised as a fully rounded character.

There may be many opportunities that pass you by, either because you are cutting people off too early, or because other people are not appreciating your qualities. Try to present yourself as a favourable figure – without being dishonest – by making your positive characteristics more obvious, and consider carefully before writing off a prospective partner yourself.

Some stereotyping has been used in this chapter for ease of representing information and because, for romantic relationships, the sexes are most attractive within their basic stereotypical roles. A man, for example, is less likely to be attracted to a woman who is aggressive and intimidating. Stereotypical male romantic qualities include:

behaving like a 'gentleman' – opening doors for the woman, letting her go into a room first, being attentive; being in control – but not taking over; being protective, strong and supportive; and not being easily flustered. Stereotypical female romantic qualities include: behaving like a 'lady' – accepting having doors opened for her, allowing the man to be attentive; and being approachable, understanding, patient, softly spoken and warm-hearted.

Although all the advice in this chapter is aimed at heterosexual relationships, in many homosexual relationships one partner takes on a more dominant role and the other a more submissive role, mimicking the ways many men and women date, so much of the advice given is still valid.

### Asking someone out

Before you can ask someone out, you need to meet someone to whom you are attracted and who finds you attractive – which you can determine from the other person's body language. Low pressured environments to meet people include the place where you work – you can get to know the person quite well before risking an invitation, evening classes, and clubs and local societies. Practise talking to as many people as you can when you are out to gain sufficient confidence to talk casually to someone you find attractive (see Chapters 5 and 6), and then to go one step further and ask for a date. However, the way in which you ask for that date could determine whether the other person accepts.

*Aggressive ways of asking someone out* include saying, 'I'm going to the new exhibition centre on Saturday. Want to come along?' The other person is not made to feel valued or wanted: you are going to the exhibition centre with or without her and you don't seem to care much whether she does accompany you.

Saying, 'How about if I treat you to an Indian meal on Saturday?' assumes too much: the other person may not consider going anywhere with you to be a treat and it sounds like you are the one doing her the favour rather than the more complimentary reverse.

*Passive ways of asking someone out* include saying, 'I was thinking about going to the new exhibition centre on Saturday but I don't like going out on my own.' Skirting around the issue risks irritating the other person: you should get to the point. Saying, 'Are you free next Saturday?' is no good either. It might be risky for the other person to admit to being free, so she might say, 'Why do you want to know?' This could make you feel more uncomfortable than if you had asked directly.

Saying, 'I don't suppose you fancy going to have a look at the new exhibition centre?' or, 'I don't expect you like Indian food?' asks with the expectation of being turned down. The other person might reply, 'What gave you that idea?' which moves the conversation away from your purpose. Even if she responds with, 'Actually, I do like Indian food,' she hasn't said yes to a date.

Asking someone out in a shy and passive way can reap rewards if the other person is as shy as you: she will feel less threatened if she thinks you are just as nervous as she is.

*Assertive ways of asking someone out* include saying, 'Would you like to come with me to the new exhibition centre on Saturday?' or, 'Would you like to go out for an Indian meal with me on Saturday?' or, 'I'd really like to see you over the weekend. Could we work something out?' You need to use assertive body language (see Chapter 8) and show that you value the other person's company, but don't make her feel pressured. Be prepared for her to turn you down. But maybe, she won't.

### The date
The first date can be crucial to your relationship because it allows time for each of you to get to know the other better.

However, there are some things to bear in mind before you even arrive.

*Safety* is a big concern when you meet someone on your own for the first time. You may barely know him or may not have even met before because, for example, you have been introduced through an agency. The other person may not be as honest as you – the person could be married – and might not be safe, whichever sex. Try to work out his motives for meeting you: is he looking for the same as you – such as a friend or long term relationship – or is he only interested in sex? If you think your date might be married try to push to meet him at a time when his family might expect him to be home such as on a Saturday night or Sunday morning: weekday only arrangements would be suspicious.

Meet in a busy place in the daytime with easy access to your home but not so close you might casually bump into the person – you don't want to risk being stalked – and so you can get home in daylight, without a need to be accompanied. Give details of your date to a friend and ask him to ring your mobile phone to check that you're OK and to expect a call from you after the date is over to say you're safe. If anything about your date worries you, don't give out your address or home telephone number or invite him back to your home or go to his place – you should wait until you know him well in any case.

*Behaviour* is important, so remind yourself before your date what things you must and must not do. Try to play down any traits your date might find intimidating or off-putting.

If you are a man, don't take a gift for your date as this will make her feel pressurised; it can also embarrass her. Likewise, don't come on too strong with letting her know that you find her attractive as it can frighten her off.

Other hindering behaviours include getting drunk, telling rude or offensive jokes, swearing, talking with a mouthful of food, and displaying annoying habits.

*Your appearance* tells the other person quite a bit about you. Dressing frumpily suggests a lack of confidence in either sex and can suggest that a man has his mother shop for him. A woman wearing tight and brief clothing and an abundance of make-up may be judged sexually experienced, as may a man exposing much of his chest and sporting jewellery, intimidating shy and unconfident people. Very short hair in either men or women can also be intimidating.

A man wearing clothing featuring cartoon characters or offensive slogans on a date shows he has not made any more effort than he would when on a night out with his mates. Under-dressing in men suggests they can't be bothered – you can always remove a jacket later to tone down over-dressing. Keep your style conventional, avoiding bright colours. A woman's clothing should be feminine, without being overtly sexy. Dressing in red and wearing red nail varnish can suggest that you are out for sex rather than romance, and wearing all black can intimidate your date.

If you are looking for a romantic attachment, and you normally fail to attract people with the characteristics you value, perhaps you are dressing to attract those who don't have them and intimidate those that do? A good way of helping you understand dress sense is by looking at other people. Note what clothes look attractive on different people and why they work for each person. Consult a style and colour book to help you choose clothes that suit you and your personality. Absolute no-nos are turning up smelly and dirty with greasy hair, and wearing clothes that are too tight with bulges of fat fighting to escape between buttons and threatening to burst zips.

*The venue* for your date should be fairly busy and friendly, rather than formal, so that both of you can relax in the environment. If possible, choose somewhere you both know. Leave going to the cinema or theatre until you have had a chance to get to know your date better and can be relaxed in such close proximity; early dates should concentrate on conversation.

### Conversation in dating

Try to find out about your date's education, work, hobbies and family – as mentioned in *Conversations with strangers* in Chapter 5. Have some other topics ready to talk about should the conversation flag to help you feel more confident before the date as well as oiling the wheels during the date. Bear in mind that the first ten minutes or so of any date can be used for discussing how long it took you to get there and where you live – without giving out your exact address, and questions about where you work – how long it takes you to travel there, how long you've been there, whether you like your job and whether you intend staying in it long.

Don't reveal too much of yourself or your life history straight away: keep bits in reserve for future meetings so that your date gradually gets to know you, keeping a part of you mysterious while not overloading him with too much information at once. For example, you may bore your date with your life story or what you say may be inappropriate – such as revealing that you were abused as a child – for someone you don't know well and with whom you have not built trust.

Show interest in your date and in what she has to say by not only talking of yourself, and show that you are following the conversation by nodding, making encouraging noises and asking questions to clarify anything you don't fully understand. Having a range of topics to talk about prevents you from getting stuck on one: brush over something that's very important to you rather than boring your date by going into great detail: that can be done at another time when you know each other better. Early conversations should be at a fairly superficial level to get a feel for the things that are important in each other's lives and if general views coincide. In-depth conversation is too heavy for a first romantic date so talking about politics is best avoided. Keep the conversation light and fun: you're there to have a good time and give your date a good time too.

Work out a couple of questions you'd like to be asked that you could ask your date, and be prepared to have them asked back: you could save these for when there is a lull in the conversation or introduce them if you feel it relevant. Suggestions are, 'Where do you see yourself in five years' time?' and, 'Have you always wanted to be a . . .?' and, 'Where's your ideal holiday destination?' However, don't use them in an interrogative way; space them out through the conversation. Be careful in your choice of questions: if you say, 'Do you like children?' or, 'When do you envisage settling down?' you are moving too fast and will scare her off.

Try to match your date's mood. If she is in a light and fun mood, try to join in so that you share the mood together. Likewise, if something more serious crops up try not to change the subject immediately or dismiss what she's said by making an insensitive remark.

Be prepared to reveal vulnerabilities, without revealing all of them at once, to help your date warm to you and identify with you. A man can feel intimidated by a woman who comes across as stronger in everything than he is, and women like to see the sensitive side of men to know they can be caring and gentle. Revealing weaknesses encourages your date to do the same and shows you to be an empathetic person who understands what it is like to have difficulties. A mutual sharing of difficulties can bind you together emotionally as you gain support from each other.

### Body language in dating

Through your body language, you need to show that you are interested in what your date has to say (see Chapters 7 and 8 for help with listening skills and interested body language) and that you find him attractive. Look for signs of your date's attraction to you to gauge how you are doing.

*Attraction* is indicated by the other person flashing his eyebrows; having more frequent and prolonged eye contact – over three seconds; increasing his blink rate; having dilated pupils; smiling a great deal, showing his teeth; mirroring your body language; laughing at your jokes; occasionally touching your arm or shoulder when he wants to laugh at a joke or emphasise a point, and having his body parts pointing towards you.

Extending his gaze from the triangle formed by your eyes, nose and mouth, to your shoulders and eventually the rest of your body, but particularly concentrating on your mouth, is a very positive sign of attraction.

*Flirting in a man* includes grooming by playing with his cuffs or lapel; removing his jacket or tie, or unbuttoning his jacket and loosening his tie, and blocking you with his body to create an intimate space that discourages others from getting near. For example, if you are both standing at a bar counter and he leans on the counter to block off one side, having his back to the rest of the room, he cuts off intrusion from anyone behind him. Or he could lean his outstretched arm on the wall against which you are leaning to block off one half of the room. Both these blocking scenarios tell other men that you are 'taken'.

*Flirting in a woman* includes grooming by playing with her hair: stroking it, flicking it back, gathering it up and letting it drop over her shoulders or letting it fall to one side to expose her neck; touching her face, neck and lips, and licking her lips, and looking askance at her date. Leaning forward to expose her cleavage or crossing her legs to reveal more thigh are also signs of flirting.

When you use body language to let your date know whether you are interested, make sure that you give clear messages and don't mix your signals or your date will be confused.

### Emotional blocks when dating

Try to be aware of emotional baggage picked up from previous relationships: don't let it interfere with you getting to know someone new. For example, if you have very low self-esteem because of what has happened to you in the past you might fear meeting someone new because you think you will be rejected. Or your manner may be so guarded and distrustful your date takes offence and decides you are not worth the effort of pursuing – which may confirm your low opinion of that sex and so spoil future chances too.

If you have unhelpful rules that hinder your getting to know others, write them down and work out how you could adapt them to suit the reality. You might believe, for example, that if a man shows interest in you, it can only mean one thing – he wants sex. Men do sometimes just want friendship or a romantic loving relationship. If you refuse all attention, you will never know what was on offer or what you missed. You need to get to know a man before you can make judgments on what he wants.

*Commitment* is about wanting to make a firm arrangement with the other person for a long-term relationship with certain expectations on either side such as being faithful and spending a great deal of time together, wanting to live together, and having children (although not all couples want children). For some it may mean marriage.

Being unable to commit is a major emotional block. Some people are fine at finding dates and stringing them out for a few weeks, even months. But, when it comes to the crunch, they are unable to go the whole way and commit to a long-term relationship. As soon as it starts to get serious they want out. They may justify this to themselves with a list of reasons, but none might be insurmountable. If this applies to you, ask yourself if you genuinely want a deep and loving relationship. If not, you should make that clear to your dates at the outset otherwise they might think you are prepared to offer more and get hurt when they realise you are not after the same things.

If you would like a deep and loving relationship but are afraid to commit ask yourself why. If you have been badly betrayed in the past, perhaps you need to go very slow with the relationship (or you might benefit from counselling). You should let your partner know what you feel and why you feel the way you do. Then perhaps you might be able to find a way through together. A lack of communication drives people apart, so you must be prepared to open up if you want to be understood and for someone to give you more time.

# 20

# CULTURAL DIFFERENCES IN SOCIAL INTERACTIONS

The code of behaviour you are given in being brought up in the West provides you with information on how to behave with others from the same cultural background. However, what may be polite to Westerners may be down-right rude to someone from another culture. And, even if speaking the same language, there can still be room for misunderstanding. This chapter is an overview of some of the most outstanding differences to the Western culture and some variations within it but is not intended as a fully comprehensive guide.

Not all the traits mentioned will be necessarily true of individuals: the information given is only useful as a general guide when dealing with large numbers from a particular culture. It must never be assumed, for example, that every Japanese person behaves in a very 'Japanese' way. That person may have been influenced by living in a major city where there is a big cultural mix or may have worked or been educated abroad. These experiences can change the way a person behaves to dilute cultural traits and to make her more 'international'.

### Culture and spoken language
Even when two cultures speak the same language, there is room for misunderstanding. Playwright George Bernard

Shaw claimed that, 'England and America are two countries divided by a common language.' Below are some examples of American English that can be open to British misinterpretation.

Americans' chips are crisps in Britain; their icebox is the refrigerator; their pants, trousers; their trunk, the car boot; their suspenders, braces; their fall, autumn. In America, a bill is a piece of paper money; in Britain, it is a piece of paper detailing what the person owes. The Americans' first floor is the ground floor in Britain; and their cart is a shopping trolley, not something pulled by horses.

British biscuits are American crackers, a British shop is an American store, and a British underground is an American subway. To the British, crackers are special dry biscuits that are eaten with cheese – or someone who is mad; a store is somewhere things are stored; and a subway is an underground passageway that's used to avoid having to cross a dangerous road.

As well as misunderstandings through different uses of the same words, Americans use some words and expressions that don't have a meaning in Britain. For example, a baby carriage is a pram, diapers are nappies, a drugstore is a chemist's, the sidewalk is the pavement, a streetcar is a tram, a traffic circle is a roundabout, a thumbtack is a drawing pin, a sack lunch is a packed lunch, and a zip code is a postcode.

With so many American films shown all over the world, many of the language differences between American and British English are picked up through the context of the action on the screen, making misunderstandings less likely. Reading books by American authors also helps close the divide.

Australian films are not as widely shown as American films, so there is less opportunity for other English speakers to learn about the nuances of speech in Australian English. Ciara wanted to drive during her visit to Australia. In group instruction, she was shocked to be told that it was illegal to drive wearing thongs, believing the instructor had referred to extremely brief women's underwear, and wondered how that affected one's driving. Later, she found out he meant flip-flops – the flat open sandals worn by gripping a post between the two largest toes.

If an Australian were to mention pavement pizza, kerbside quiche, liquid laugh, rainbow sneeze, Technicolor yawn or driving the porcelain bus, would you know what he was talking about? Vomit.

### Jokes

Even within your own culture, you have to choose your audience well when telling a joke and it can take some skill to deliver the punch line artfully. So to take that joke to any other culture is asking for trouble.

At best, it can fall flat as my jokes did when I was at school, believing I could take Hungarian humour from home and share it with my friends. Only after I had told one joke three times in an effort for my friends to appreciate the humour did I realise that they just couldn't see the funny side and never would. From then on, if I said I had a joke to tell, there would be groans of, 'Not another Hungarian joke' and the laughter that followed was not for the joke but for how bad they thought it was.

After living for 55 years in the UK, my Hungarian father still has trouble appreciating some British jokes.

At worst, you can seriously offend someone when telling a joke. Jokes with any sexual content, for example, would utterly embarrass anyone from South East Asia where sex talk is taboo. Many jokes are racist or sexist and you can easily offend with these too. So it is best to avoid telling jokes altogether; they just don't travel.

### Meeting and greeting people from around the world

Wherever you are, it is important to be able to remember, and accurately pronounce, someone's name – if you haven't caught it exactly you can ask the other person to repeat it and to correct any mispronunciation on your part. If your own name has ever been mispronounced, you will appreciate how it jars and should someone have difficulty recalling your name you do wonder whether they remember anything else about you. I have often asked someone to spell his or her name for me so that I can better picture how it should sound and it helps me to remember it for the next time: I have often privately made a note of the phonetic sounds so that I can recreate the name when necessary. Even if you never get it perfect, showing that you have made an effort would be welcomed. You should also find out the polite form of address, as the level of formality required is not always clear. If you blunder this early on, it may be hard to regain ground later.

In arranging to meet someone, it is good to remember that in the West, punctuality is important but in many Latin American countries, Spain, Portugal and Arab countries, people are often late. Keeping people waiting in South East Asia will result in them losing face – which is taboo.

There are differences in personal space around the world too. Westerners tend to like talking at arm's length to people they don't know well but in Arab countries and Latin America people like to stand and sit closer than they do in the West; people from these countries can be a great deal more tactile than Westerners too.

The manner in which people greet you depends on where in the world they are from and how intimately you know them. The information given below is for people who do not know each other well or are meeting for the first time in their own country.

North Americans and Australians often have very strong, albeit brief, handshakes. In South East Asia people usually bow from the waist and don't shake hands unless they are used to dealing with Westerners and then they may do both. The degree of the bow is related to how superior or subordinate to themselves they consider you to be and is a sign of humility; so people from these countries may ask questions to determine which of you is higher on the social scale. When Asians and South East Asians do shake hands, they gently clasp the hand without any pressure and very little pumping; but they hold the handshake longer than Westerners. It is taboo to touch a person's head, such as in greeting a child, in much of South East Asia as the head is considered sacred by Buddhists. When greeting a Russian, you must not shake hands or kiss over the threshold of a doorway as it is considered bad luck.

Italians greet other people with warm enthusiastic handshakes. Germans have a brief handshake and the French have a light grip, giving it a single, quick shake. In Columbia, men shake hands often while grasping the other's forearm or elbow at the same time; women frequently just hold forearms instead of shaking hands. In Chile, women often pat the other woman's right forearm or shoulder. In the Philippines, they do shake hands but it is also common to greet each other with an eyebrow flash. Arab men may greet other men by grasping right hands, holding the other's shoulder with their left hands and kissing on both cheeks; but they may not touch women. Although it is quite usual in much of South East Asia, Arab countries and Turkey for two men or two women to walk holding hands or having arms around each other in friendship, members of the opposite sex do not touch in public.

There can also be variations in greeting depending on whether the woman is a traditional Muslim or an Orthodox Jew: in their native countries, such as in the Middle East or Asia, their religious husbands may not introduce them to another man and in those circumstances the polite thing to do is to ignore the wives as the husbands do. Even if you are introduced to someone's wife, it is safer to see if she initiates a handshake – many Muslim women will not want to shake a male hand. Some Muslim men won't want to shake hands with you if you are female and may see you as inviting sexual attention if you do initiate a handshake – yet in the West, it is often the woman who is expected to initiate the handshake. Some Orthodox Jewish people might not want to shake hands with anyone from the opposite gender and many Indian and Thai women also choose not to shake hands, preferring you to bow slightly with palms together as in prayer – so take your cue from them.

### Body language variations around the world

*Unconscious body gestures* that accompany speech tend to be the same all over the world – such as smiling when you're pleased to see someone. However, in Greece, people also smile when they are upset or angry and, in much of Asia, a smile can also be used to cover up embarrassment, shock or anger; many South East Asians often giggle to cover up embarrassment.

*Conscious body gestures* have a specific meaning within the culture they are used. For example, to communicate with someone who's too far away to hear, people from the West often meet index finger and thumb together for the OK sign while the remaining fingers point upwards. But in Arab countries, Italy, Brazil and Germany it is a sign of obscenity, similar to the raised middle finger in the West that says 'up yours'; in Turkey, it can signify that someone is homosexual. In Korea, China and Japan the gesture means money. In France, the gesture is used to indicate zero or that something is worthless; if you take that circle of thumb and forefinger and then place it over your nose while turning that circle around the outside of your nose, you are saying that a person is drunk. In Columbia, putting the circle over your nose says that a person is homosexual.

The thumbs-up sign in Britain and North America means everything is OK or it can mean you are thumbing a lift. But in Arab countries, Spain, Australia and Brazil it is considered an obscene gesture: 'sit on this'. But if you put your thumb up in Japan, you are indicating the number five. In the Netherlands, people suck their thumb to signal that someone is lying; in Britain, people suck their thumb to suggest someone is behaving like a baby.

Holding your index and second fingers up in a 'V' with your palm facing inwards is an obscene gesture in Britain. In Arab countries, punching an open palm into the fist of your other hand, then quickly running it down to the elbow, while the elbow moves up, gives the same meaning. In Russia and Hungary, the gesture is translated similarly but with a horse's anatomy in mind rather than a man's.

In Britain, you 'keep your fingers crossed' to wish someone good luck, yet in Germany they 'press thumbs' by making fists around them and then moving the base of their closed fists up and down as though to thump a surface. The gesture of placing a thumb between the first and second fingers of a fist, widely known as 'the fig', represents female genitals and is considered obscene in most of the world but in Portugal, Venezuela and Brazil it is a sign to give protection or to bring good luck – it had been believed that evil spirits would be distracted by being shown sexual organs and so could do no harm. In Arab countries, men use 'the fig' to insult another person, of either sex.

Throughout the world, people indicate something in a variety of ways. Using your index finger to point, as is the custom in most of the West, is considered very rude in Arab countries and South East Asia. The thrust of the chin is used to point in some African cultures; a pursing of the lips while staring in the same direction is used in the

Philippines; in much of South East Asia, they use an open hand and in Indonesia and Malaysia, they point with the thumb.

Holding your palm up in any manner to face someone in Greece means that you want to shove excrement into the other person's face. So to wave, hail a cab, say thanks to a fellow driver, or use the gesture to tell the other person to stop or go back, is inadvisable in Greece. In Chile, holding up an outwardly facing palm with fingers spread implies the other person is stupid.

Beckoning people with an upward palm using just the index finger or the more enthusiastic gesture using all fingers is common in the West. But it is considered rude in most of Africa, South East Asia and much of Asia: people beckon using all fingers in the same way as in the West with one major difference – their palms face downward. This could be misinterpreted in the West as a gesture to send you away or for you to move back. In Scandinavian countries, people beckon with a toss of the head.

South East Asians may show disagreement by squinting or sucking in air through their teeth, as they don't like to say no. In Bulgaria and Greece, shaking the head means yes and nodding means no – the opposite of other Western cultures. In Turkey, a sharp downward nod of the head means a definite yes, and a slow downward movement is a less sure yes. An upward jerk of the head means no; doing this with raised eyebrows and a tut, achieved by sucking the tongue against the top palate, means a very definite no. Staring sternly at someone while shaking the head up and down is a warning gesture for him to stop what he is doing or there will be consequences; shaking the head from side to side shows disbelief or astonishment. To gesture no in Taiwan, people lift their hand to their face, palm outwards, and let it swing from side to side like a windscreen wiper.

Don't rely on body gestures alone to give a specific message, unless it is to someone from the same cultural background as you, or you may be seriously misunderstood. And be aware that many countries also have taboo body language with regard to polite social behaviour such as how close you should stand to the person you are talking to. In many countries, it is considered rude and disrespectful to talk with your hands in your pockets, or to shake hands with someone while your other hand is in your pocket or to bow with hands in pockets. And in many parts of the world, it is considered aggressive to talk to someone with folded arms or with hands on hips.

### Taboos and customs

Taboos are forbidden behaviours or subjects for conversation related to culture or religion: if you break a taboo, great offence will be given. Sometimes a taboo is shared generally with other countries such as discussing toilet habits and bowel movements at the table, eating with your mouth open, leaning back while propping shoed feet on tables or chairs, chewing gum while talking to someone, being loud in public and becoming very drunk as a guest in someone's home or at a formal occasion. Other taboos are peculiar to an individual country (such as not stepping on a doorsill in Thailand as it is considered bad luck), or group of countries (such as not serving beef to Hindus, or pork or alcohol to Muslims – although less strict Muslims do drink alcohol).

*Table manners* in Arab countries, Pakistan, parts of Africa, Malaysia and Indonesia, where they are predominantly Muslim, demand that you don't eat with your left hand: this is reserved for cleaning your bottom and is considered unclean even when washed. (If you are left-handed, tell the host before you start eating and remember not to eat with your right hand.) Neither must you shake hands with your left hand or offer a gift with your left hand. These strictures also apply to Hindus.

Some things that are taboo in the West are loudly

smacking your lips and belching while at the table, yet are considered complimentary by people in Korea and other parts of South East Asia. It is neither a compliment nor an offence to belch in Arab countries; it is something that is sometimes done and no one thinks any the worse of you.

In some parts of South East Asia, Israel and North Africa, it is rude to empty your plate completely as this suggests you have not had enough to eat. But in many other parts of the world leaving food on your plate is rude as it suggests you don't like it or that you were greedy and took more than you could eat – someone might say that your eyes are bigger than your stomach.

Any mention of being hungry, even when presented with a table laden with food, is taboo for Arabs and South East Asians. Yet among friends in Britain, it is complimentary to say you are hungry before the meal as it shows an eagerness to eat plenty of what you are offered thereby complimenting the host. Although you may not voice your hunger or show eagerness at the table in Arab countries and South East Asia, you are expected to eat what you are offered or what is put before you: to not do so would give offence.

Going to the toilet during a meal in France and the Netherlands is considered rude. If you have to go to the toilet during a meal in Arab countries it signifies the end of your meal – you may re-join the others at the table but you must not eat anything else as you are now considered unclean.

To fart at the table when eating with Arabs or Turks is an outrage. Your fellow diners would fall silent, try not to meet your eyes and only slowly would conversation resume. The perpetrator can expect never to be invited to eat at that house again – and, if word gets round, he may be shunned from other households too. Very young children and babies are excused from this protocol. The reason this is taboo for Muslims is that, for them, the concept of eating is holy and you should be thankful to God for what you have before you – so going to the toilet mid-meal or farting shows a lack of respect for their values as both these acts are considered unclean, defiling the food on the table.

*Polite conversation* with Arabs includes avoiding asking after another man's wife, but enquiring after male members of his family specifically or making a general enquiry about his family or children. There is no restriction on a woman enquiring after the health of another woman.

You should avoid any sort of confrontation or discussion of contentious issues with South East Asians and Arabs and must not openly criticise someone: it is of vital importance to them that they do not lose face.

*Feet* can cause offence. In Arab countries, South East Asia, India, Turkey, Hungary and Russia, your shoes must be removed inside the person's home and in some Arab countries and in much of South East Asia, it is rude to show the soles of your feet. In South East Asia and India, you must not point with your foot or use it to touch an object, as feet are considered dirty.

*Giving and receiving gifts* has many pitfalls. When accepting a gift in Arab countries and in South East Asia, it is polite to be hesitant and you should not be over-effusive in your thanks: these things will make you appear greedy. However, you must show pleasure by smiling and graciously thanking the giver. You must never open the gift in front of the other person in case your expression shows a negative response such as disappointment or puzzlement; opening the gift immediately would also make you appear greedy. There is also the risk that the giver loses face if the gift for you is not as valuable as the one you gave him.

When you give a gift in South East Asia, unlike with Muslim and Hindu cultures where the right hand only will do, you must present it using both hands, playing down its importance – and it should not be worth more than any gift you have been given. If the other person initially refuses the gift, she is showing modesty and you need to offer it again and perhaps even a third time. Then it will be graciously accepted.

Since only the wrappings can be admired, the gift should be wrapped very carefully. Red and pink are the preferred colours with South East Asians as they are meant to be auspicious, but white is taboo as it is associated with funerals – so is the giving of handkerchiefs. In China, the colours blue and black are also associated with funerals. Bright coloured wrapping paper is appreciated in Thailand but in Japan, pastels are better. Don't write any message in red as Buddhists only have their name written in red when they are dead and it symbolises the ending of the relationship; ensure any cards you give or send aren't red either. Giving four of something in Japan and Korea is also associated with death. Giving any sharp object such as scissors, a knife or a letter opener symbolises the cutting of the relationship.

You must not give leather goods to Hindus as the cow is sacred to them and, if you give leather goods to Muslims, you must stress that it is cow hide and not pig leather you are giving. In Japan, flowers are only given at funerals, as a get-well gift and during courtship. In Russia and Germany, it is polite to give an odd number of flowers as even numbers are for funerals.

*Blowing your nose* in public in Arab countries and South East Asia is considered rude, especially if done at the table. In South East Asia, you should not use cloth handkerchiefs but disposable tissues – and once a tissue has been used it must be thrown away, not saved for later use.

*Assertiveness* in many cultures, especially in women, is not considered desirable. Very often people of either sex in South East Asia do not want to make eye contact, and it is considered rude for women to initiate conversation. In

South East Asia, it is also considered rude to say no and the word yes may actually mean yes, maybe or even no. The listener is expected to tell from the level of enthusiasm which meaning to apply.

In the West, assertiveness is considered a very worthwhile skill and necessary for good relationships in and out of work but we cannot heavy-handedly impose Western values on any other culture: although we have every right to change ourselves, we have no right to change other people.

If you are going to be dealing with someone from another culture, try to find out about taboos and expected behaviour so that you don't offend the other person. Copy the behaviour of the other person where possible – so if he doesn't slouch nor must you; if he eats his bread with a knife and fork, always has his hands on the table while eating or leaves food on his plate, so must you. If you think you've broken a taboo, ask if this is the case and apologise, explaining that it is acceptable in your culture and you hadn't known there would be a difference.

# INDEX

## MAKE YOUR WILL THE RIGHT WAY

Have you made a will? Or have you 'somehow' not got round to it yet? If the latter, you need this book.

All of us aged 18 and above should make a will to ensure that our property is shared out according to our own wishes after our death. If you don't leave a will, your property will be divided up according to the laws of intestacy – which probably won't be what you want!

Solicitor Joyce Bennell shares her 28 years of experience of will-writing to show how to make a valid will, including choosing appropriate executors and making sure that the will is properly witnessed.

## DIVORCE
## THE THINGS YOU THOUGHT YOU'D
## NEVER NEED TO KNOW

Nobody marries with divorce in mind. So if our marriage breaks down, we are disillusioned, upset and unprepared. But we have to face difficult decisions. With this book, Jill Black QC and Elizabeth Auckland steer us calmly and sympathetically, and in the right order, through what can be a 'minefield'.

A broad insight into how courts make their decisions – especially regarding the children, the home and finances – helps us appreciate what to expect in our own circumstances. Tax considerations are also dealt with.

# RIGHT WAY
# PUBLISHING POLICY

## HOW WE SELECT TITLES

**RIGHT WAY** consider carefully every deserving manuscript. Where an author is an authority on his subject but an inexperienced writer, we provide first-class editorial help. The standards we set make sure that every **RIGHT WAY** book is practical, easy to understand, concise, informative and delightful to read. Our specialist artists are skilled at creating simple illustrations which augment the text wherever necessary.

## CONSISTENT QUALITY

At every reprint our books are updated where appropriate, giving our authors the opportunity to include new information.

## FAST DELIVERY

We sell **RIGHT WAY** books to the best bookshops throughout the world. It may be that your bookseller has run out of stock of a particular title. If so, he can order more from us at any time – we have a fine reputation for ''same day'' despatch, and we supply any order, however small (even a single copy), to any bookseller who has an account with us. We prefer you to buy from your bookseller, as this reminds him of the strong underlying public demand for **RIGHT WAY** books. However, you can order direct from us by post or by phone with a credit card.

## FREE

If you would like an up-to-date list of all **RIGHT WAY** titles currently available, please send a stamped self-addressed envelope to ELLIOT RIGHT WAY BOOKS, BRIGHTON ROAD, LOWER KINGSWOOD, TADWORTH, SURREY, KT20 6TD, U.K. or visit our website at **www.right-way.co.uk**